the *Artistic* Mother

by Shona Cole

A PRACTICAL
GUIDE TO FITTING
CREATIVITY INTO
YOUR BUSY LIFE

NORTH LIGHT BOOKS
Cincinnati, Ohio

www.mycraftivity.com

14 13 12 11 10   5 4 3 2 1

DISTRIBUTED IN CANADA BY FRASER DIRECT
100 Armstrong Avenue
Georgetown, ON, Canada L7G 5S4
Tel: (905) 877-4411

DISTRIBUTED IN THE U.K. AND EUROPE BY DAVID & CHARLES
Brunel House, Newton Abbot, Devon, TQ12 4PU, England
Tel: (+44) 1626 323200, Fax: (+44) 1626 323319
Email: postmaster@davidandcharles.co.uk

DISTRIBUTED IN AUSTRALIA BY CAPRICORN LINK
P.O. Box 704, S. Windsor NSW, 2756 Australia
Tel: (02) 4577-3555

Library of Congress Cataloging in Publication Data
Cole, Shona, 1972-
  The artistic mother : a practical guide to fitting creativity into your busy life
/ Shona Cole.
    p. cm.
Includes bibliographical references and index.
ISBN-13: 978-1-60061-348-7 (alk. paper)
ISBN-10: 1-60061-348-9 (alk. paper)
1. Motherhood. 2. Creative ability. 3. Time management. I. Title.
HQ759.C683 2010
306.874'3--dc22
                    2009028411

fw media
www.fwmedia.com

Edited by Liz Casler
Designed by Marissa Bowers
Production coordinated by Greg Nock
Photo styling by Jan Nickum
Photography by Christine Polomsky and David Peterson

Metric Conversion Chart

TO CONVERT	TO	MULTIPLY BY
Inches	Millimeters	25.4
Millimeters	Inches	0.04
Inches	Centimeters	2.54
Centimeters	Inches	0.4
Feet	Centimeters	30.5
Centimeters	Feet	0.03
Yards	Meters	0.9
Meters	Yards	1.1
Sq. Inches	Sq. Centimeters	6.45
Sq. Centimeters	Sq. Inches	0.16
Sq. Feet	Sq. Meters	0.09
Sq. Meters	Sq. Feet	10.8
Sq. Yards	Sq. Meters	0.8
Sq. Meters	Sq. Yards	1.2
Pounds	Kilograms	0.45
Kilograms	Pounds	2.2
Ounces	Grams	28.3
Grams	Ounces	0.035

About the Author

As I grew up in Dublin, Ireland, I was drawn to the arts. I took poetry, watercolor, oil and life drawing classes after school and in the evenings while in college. Before I had children I was determined to follow a "proper" career path. I received my M.A. in psychology from the University of Dublin, Trinity College, and focused on a career in social services. During those years I spent little time creating art. But when I was pregnant with my first child, I quit work and began to decorate the nursery. It was then that I rediscovered my love of painting and discovered crafting. I have been creating ever since.

My husband Mark and I are the proud parents of five children: Matthew, 10, Lily Kate, 8, Laura, 6, Annie Rose, 4 and Max, 1. We live in a rambling ranch house nestled on five acres an hour north of Houston, Texas, with lots of dogs, singing, painting and books.

I spend my days homeschooling my children, recording everything with a lens and a pen. I spend my nights making art in my craft room next to the kitchen. My art gives me a sense of self, purpose and beauty as a woman and as a mother. I have experienced many ups and downs as a mother. I am a good mom some days and I am crabby and overwhelmed on others. But I am committed to striving to be better each day. I have noticed a pattern: The longer I walk a committed artistic path, the fewer "bad Momma" days I seem to have!

This book is a compilation of all I have learned over the years in becoming a functioning Artistic Mother while not neglecting my motherly duties. I hope you can glean something from my words, and I wish you all the best as you explore art and find inspiration and beauty as you raise your precious children.

Acknowledgments

Thank you to my husband and constant companion, Mark, for everything. To my children, for being such beautiful, creative, interesting souls. To my Mum for unfailing support and help. To my Dad for giving me oil paints when I was a girl and always believing in me. To Erin Lichnovsky who was the inspiration for the book. To the artists spotlighted in this book: Shannon Mucha, Corey Moortgat, Rebecca Sower, Misty Mawn, Susan Tuttle, Ellene McClay and Audrey Hernandez, thank you for your generosity and commitment to your children and art and for inspiring me to be better at both. To the artists who contributed to the book: Shelley Kommers, Mendy Mitrani, Carrie Harney, Sarah Keith and Cindy Mayfield. To Tonia Davenport for giving me this opportunity. To Liz Casler for her invaluable guidance and dedication. To Christine Polomsky for her wonderful photography. To Marissa Bowers for her artful design work. To North Light Books for their creative vision and commitment to the arts. To Jenny Doh for being supportive of my art from the very beginning. I would not be here without you.

To those artists who have shared their knowledge in the books I have devoured: Claudine Hellmuth, Karen Michel, Michelle Ward, Lynne Perrella and Nita Leland. To poets who have spoken volumes to me: Claudia Emerson, B.H. Fairchild, Billy Collins and Ted Kooser.

Contents

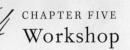

Workshop

DEDICATION

To the Mothers
who are also
artistic souls.

the backdoor squeaks delight in her
passing. I follow just to see
her crouching, fingers in the dirt,
she finds the wriggle of a worm
beneath fallen leaves

her knees stain

Annie loves drawing!

Introduction

Why Should Mothers Make Time to Create Art?

Ah, motherhood. What a journey! It can be simultaneously exciting and exhausting, demanding and rewarding, frustrating and glorious! No matter the age of our children, whether little ones grace our homes—tugging at our skirts, constantly needing us—or our children are older—kids or teens needing space, guidance and friendship—life is noisy, complicated and busy. As moms we serve, guide, cuddle, entertain, teach, groom and nurture our children. Along with listening to their ideas and struggles, moms pour out tenderness and mercy, orange juice and Cheerios (sometimes it seems all at once!). We work harder at motherhood than we ever realized we would.

And what a tremendous responsibility it is! How we raise these budding human beings affects who they become as adults. Our parenting styles and personalities rub off on our children. When we become moms we walk into a job that is vitally important to the world.

Faced with busy-ness and a sense of great responsibility, moms often overdo it, giving sacrificially until there is nothing left. No one—not us, not our children—benefits if we become burned out, miserable or exhausted. In order to avoid traveling down that stressful road, we need to bring some balance to our lives and keep the batteries of our souls charged. Taking time to create art can help.

Creating art leads to a glorious sense of personal fulfillment. When we have a project germinating in our minds, or a new bolt of fabric on our worktable, or our latest photos ready to be processed, we experience a surge of motivation, anticipation and excitement. While we work through art projects, kneading the ideas and feeling the brushstrokes, the joy of creating makes us feel alive and refreshed. And when we put down the glue stick, stand back from our creation and know it is finished, we can bask in a sense of accomplishment. The sense of well-being and fulfillment our creativity generates often spills over into other areas of life, including our mothering.

Creating art also enriches our perspective on our lives as mothers. As we develop artistically we become more attentive to our surroundings, thoughts and feelings. Details begin to matter more. We learn to focus on the important and the beautiful in ourselves and our kids. Over time, through the creative process, we learn to love life a little more, embrace the beauty in the mundane, see more good in the world and take greater pleasure in whom our children are becoming.

More importantly, creating art has a positive influence on our children's lives and the lives of others. Our commitment to and creation of art communicates our vision and values to our children. Seeing us create inspires them to follow our lead, experiment with art, or at least gain an appreciation for the arts. When friends and family visit, artwork communicates our personal style, dreams and desires while providing a jumping-off point for conversation. Just as attending art exhibits or looking at photographs inspires us, our artwork inspires friends and family to create or purchase art themselves.

Creativity is a gift to be received, opened and enjoyed to the fullest. As artistic souls, it serves us well to own the gift of creativity and carve out the time and space to work at it and produce art. Rather than stealing from the energy we use as mothers, the time devoted to art makes mothering more vibrant. By coupling our maternal instincts with our creative actions, we become well-rounded women with a positive outlook—and therefore content, hopeful and happy mothers. Don't you want to love your life a little more tomorrow than you do today?

"What art offers is space— a certain breathing room for the spirit."

JOHN UPDIKE

About This Book

Some days creative ideas flow easily. Perhaps, after reading an inspiring art magazine or attending a class on papermaking, the flow of ideas is endless and the desire to make something is urgent and strong. When motivation is highest it is easy to make the time for artistic pursuits. Other days, however, we feel flat, uninspired and uninterested. Reality can be very uninspiring at times, and the tyranny of the urgent pulls our attention away from the beauty of life, often causing us to lose touch with our creative side and wearing us out. We could be doing a little artwork, but the motivation is just not strong enough. The house needs to be cleaned and the pantry shelves restocked; upset or excited kids need attention; a deadline at work is looming. Life has its seasons. When there is an illness in the family, a difficult pregnancy, a family vacation or some other event or issue, art may have to take a back seat. I know—I have been there! But when it comes to the regular busyness of everyday life, we can find ways to squeeze out the time and motivation we need to attend to our creative selves.

I have five children under the age of ten and have faced many of the daily constraints that you have. I have had times of both creative feast and famine. But I have learned over the years to see art in the precious details of daily life, taking note of the little things my children say and do, so when the feast times reappear I have images and concepts to draw from and express. Similarly, I have learned to keep my hand in the creative pot even in small ways so my skills do not become rusty.

In this book, I provide some powerful but commonsense tools that I hope you can apply to your life in order to help you prioritize and focus your days, weeks and years so the art you dream of gets done and your creative muscles get some exercise. Take these tools, make a plan, execute the plan and get it done. I want to help you!

Imagine I am your girlfriend. Let's get together for a play date. The kids can play while we chat. We can tell each other how we are managing in our crazy, busy lives. Let me tell you how I have learned to live a life composed of artmaking and children, and how I find the time and motivation to fill my home with handmade things, poetic words and a beautiful record of the details of my life as a mother. Let me show you some of the art pieces I have made and tell

long days, late nights

thankfully, her happy breath now winter
in this yellow afternoon sunlight

I remember her hands holding
the measure of all I have seen, have been, will be

her running with sharp objects
her climbing on top of bookshelves, chest of drawers

her dancing close, her relentless emerging
her wildheart, her slight journey

I can never tell which way her mood will go
any minute now she will demand a spoon for yoghurt

mint clouds in a bowl
hungry for other nothings, music, sweet liquid

for fake roses to decorate her bedroom, sheets of paper,
markers, she will find are dried out from the absence of caps

a glass sleep is here, her late light cry
and then finally in the dark sky - silence

you how you can make them, too, using simple, doable techniques and readily available art and craft supplies.

I am what you would call a jack-of-all-trades—I love all kinds of art: photography, painting, collage and poetry. I have tried to live without each of them but failed miserably. So I continue to try my hand at many different art media. I have learned to follow my heart and interests. Of course, you will have your own style and particular poetic leanings and ideas. My hope is that you will take what I have to say home with you and try it out, personalizing it for your version of motherhood and artistry.

The first three chapters of this book define creativity and break it down into a step-by-step process. In chapter one, I focus on the meaning of creativity, demystifying the creative process and demonstrating how art can fit realistically into daily life. Chapter two outlines some practical tools to use to maintain creative motivation. Chapter three addresses some commonsense ways to organize time so there is space for creativity in your busy schedule.

In chapter four, I introduce three art disciplines: photography, poetry and mixed-media art. These can form the basis for a beautiful creative expression for mothers. This section contains a quick overview of the tools, techniques and ideas used in each of the disciplines, as well as ideas as to how they can be combined to make the art projects in the last chapter of the book.

Chapter five contains a twelve-week workshop I developed to guide busy moms through making an array of family-focused art pieces. Since the goal of this workshop is for you to actually complete the projects, each week has an easy-to-follow day-by-day schedule, and every project can be created using a limited number of easy-to-find art supplies and simple techniques.

Scattered throughout the book you will find short artist spotlights highlighting the life and work of other artistic mothers who have made a commitment to produce art while raising children. These mothers have willingly given us a peek inside their lives in order to share insights to motivate us to live similarly art-filled lives. Be prepared to be inspired!

So, the front porch is waiting. The sun is shining. The kids are content. Let's talk!

These days I'm often walking out on

the stones, face to heaven looking to

see if there is the slightest chance of rain.

1 Understanding Creativity

You may have learned to believe, as I once did, that creativity belongs only to the chosen few who have special talent, inspiration and huge blocks of uninterrupted time—not to a busy mother living with the daily realities of diapers and tantrums, chores and work. When the demands of real life mute your creative desires or when you don't feel like doing art all the time that belief is reinforced. Then, if you do get around to creating something, it may not look right the first time so you become your own worst critic, sabotaging your ideas and visions with negative I-am-no-good-at-this self-talk. But there is hope!

In this chapter I break creativity down and show you that the creative process, like motherhood, involves planning and prioritizing, time and energy, imagination and dreaming, commitment and action. For a mother, this is all familiar territory that, once applied to your artistic life, is both accessible and doable.

"Creativity is the ability to make or bring into existence something new."
WEBSTER'S DICTIONARY

The Creative Process

There are moments of creative enlightenment—the aha! moments—when the thrill of producing a new idea or image becomes tangible. Perhaps the crayons you find in your purse inspire you to envision the color scheme for a new set of cards, or your son's too-small superhero costume makes you want to write a poem about the evanescent nature of time. These moments are fleeting and are truly the stuff of joy. But the process of creating involves more than just those moments. There are many essential activities that make up a full, creative life—many steps you must take before that set of cards is made or that poem written. Some of those steps are mundane, such as going to the store to buy the cardstock, jotting down descriptive words or preparing your work space for crafting, and are often not considered to be particularly creative. But in reality, artists work every day on many subsidiary activities that move them constantly toward the final products of creative accomplishment. These numerous smaller activities comprise what is widely known as the *creative process*. The activities of the creative process fall

roughly into four stages: imagining and research, preparation, project execution and resolution. When we create, we can expect to go through each of these stages. Some we will zip through quickly, while we may languish in others for days, weeks and sometimes years.

STAGE 1:
Imagining and Research

During the stage of imagining and research, the artist thinks about the project and formulates ideas and images. Imagining can happen anytime—before or just after sleep, when doing humdrum tasks such as folding laundry, when resting or when engaged in creative activities such as writing or taking photographs. It includes any time spent focused on generating new ideas, themes, color schemes or deciding what we want to focus our creative energy on. To imagine new ideas or concepts we must remain open to possibilities, reserve judgment, brainstorm, be flexible and actively look for new combinations of colors, concepts, words or images.

Some form of research generally accompanies imagination. Research is an important way to gather information to feed creative vision, imagination and know-how. It can mean looking at the work of other artists, reading how-to books and magazines, taking classes or review-

ing our journal or idea files. Without research, we may never know the extent to which we can stretch our skills and ideas. Research can also mean taking the time to really see the details of life—the shapes, sounds and colors of our days and the people gracing them. To seek out the content for art we need to slow down and listen, look and experience life. Reflection allows art to be truly authentic. As moms we often don't have the luxury of waiting for the perfect time to reflect, so we need to train ourselves to be inspired by our children in the midst of our daily lives.

STAGE 2: Preparation

During the preparation stage, the artist gathers, purchases or acquires the tools and supplies necessary to produce artwork, perhaps pillaging art supply drawers, checking on paint levels or taking a trip to the craft store. We might write the first draft of a poem or sift through photos for images with great composition or lighting. This is also the time to plan the steps of a project, organize time in which to work, clear a space to create and even do small tasks such as cleaning brushes or trimming images.

STAGE 3:
Project Execution

During the execution phase of the creative process, the artist actively engages in painting, writing, photographing or other creative acts with the intent of creating a piece of artwork. It's time to execute the envisioned plan. Sometimes it is enough to simply follow the plan we've already laid out. Other

times a theme can be developed further, changing the direction of the idea, and creating or generating new images or ideas.

STAGE 4: Resolution

Resolution involves knowing when to stop, put down the stamp pad and step away from the craft table. It is a time to print out your words or images, or hang your art on the wall. It is a time to evaluate and learn so the next time you can make similar or better choices in your art making. The more you work on art, the easier it is to recognize the end of a project. In the meantime, simply let your intuition tell you when to call it a day.

"Crank out as many experimental riffs as possible. Your style will emerge as you become a student of your own processes."

SUZANNE SIMANAITIS

SKILL DEVELOPMENT AND PERSONAL STYLE

Artistic skill goes hand in hand with artistic creativity. Skills are the practical tools necessary to bring an idea to fruition. You acquire skills through education and practice. Anyone willing to put in the time can learn artistic skills—busy moms included! However, you have to apply yourself if you truly want to improve your skills.

Skills can be learned through imitation. At the start of a creative journey you must take time to learn the tools of the trade from others. Imitate the styles, ideas, color choices and so on of artists whose work you admire. When you have worked on your creative and artistic skills for a while you will develop your own unique style by blending together the things you have learned from others.

Learning From the Wise

Have you read the tortoise and the hare fable to your children? The one about the slow tortoise beating the zippy, overly confident, nap-taking hare in a race? Fables are designed to teach children life lessons. Let's take a page from Tortoise's book and apply the lessons to our understanding of creativity.

Small Steps

Tortoise walked step-by-step until he reached the finish line. To become good at something we must work at it day in, day out, bit by bit. We do not have to wait for huge blocks of time before we can get something done. Unlike Tortoise, we are not in a race. We do not have to write a book or create a body of work by tomorrow! With even an hour each day, if we are consistent, we can improve our skills and make the art we desire to create.

Planning

Tortoise used his time wisely and kept on with the race. You may feel that your time is not your own—that it is controlled by your children's needs and desires. To some extent it is, but there are pockets of time that are truly yours. You can use them productively or unproductively. Align your priorities and act on them in a purposeful manner to get things done.

Feelings

When Tortoise saw Hare race on ahead, he could have felt dejected and given up, but he kept going. You may feel like you will never get anything done or that your skills will never improve. You may feel like giving up. But you must persist regardless of those feelings. Also, stop waiting to feel like doing art and just do it. Waiting until you feel like doing art will not gain you the skills needed to produce something you want to hang on the walls of your home. Achievement comes with commitment and self-discipline.

Labeling

Everyone knows tortoises are slow. Even so, Tortoise decided to race.

You may have never learned to see yourself as an artist. Perhaps no one will label you as such if you are not showing in galleries or publishing books of poems. Don't let that keep you from creating. Give yourself permission to live creatively anyhow. If you do what artists do, integrating art into your mothering day in and day out, seeing your daily life as beautiful and inspiring, eventually you may very well bear that title!

Self-Criticism

Tortoise could have succumbed to self-criticism at any point and given up. When you start out on the crafting path, you may judge your shortcomings so harshly that you end up packing away the art supplies. But if you push on, your skills will improve. Agree to stop second-guessing yourself, replacing self-criticism with self-evaluation.

"No matter how daunting it may feel sometimes, small steps are what it takes to really live...one step at a time...one layer at a time, as we live each moment... deliberately, authentically and passionately."

JENNY DOH

Be Like Tortoise and Not Like Hare!

As a mom and an artist you have to set a goal and plan your time, accepting that sometimes the art time you have may be devoted to doing mundane but essential art-related tasks. Work to maintain a positive attitude so you can focus on your art and be ready when the muse blows your way.

SELF-CRITICISM IN ACTION

Many years ago I painted children's stools. Friends started asking me to make them for their kids, too. After doing some simple designs I tried to come up with different and more elaborate styles, but the stools took me a long time to create and didn't look as good as I had hoped. Even though my friends were pleased with what I gave them, I was disappointed in myself and eventually threw up my hands and quit painting stools.

This is a clear case of the destructive force of self-criticism. I repeated the mantra, "I am not creative or good enough," thus sabotaging my future work by robbing myself of motivation. The reality was that I lacked skill, which takes time and effort to develop. If I had stuck with it and had reasonable expectations I could have improved and found a way to paint what I desired.

JUST DO IT

After I had my first child I found I had gained a few extra pounds. My friend Julie and I each purchased the same six-week in-home exercise video program. We followed it closely in our respective homes, keeping each other accountable, and started to lose the weight. The program was pretty tough and many days we just didn't feel like exercising. Julie explained to me one day how she kept it going:

She told herself each day that today she would not do the program. She told herself that even as she pulled on her exercise clothes and even as she put the DVD in the player and even as she pressed play. The bright, cheerful instructor would come on and Julie would tell herself she would just do the warm-up, and then just the cardio and then just the upper body and then...somehow she would have reached the yoga and cool-down segment! Doing art is like our experience with the video. Sometimes you just have to show up no matter how uninspired you feel. Override your feelings and start. It will be worth it in the end!

"Self-discipline is the road to creative freedom. Get control of yourself and your environment, and your creative spirit will flourish. Be a self-starter. No one will do it for you.... Think positively. You can do it, if you think you can."

NITA LELAND

Shannon Mucha

NUMBER OF CHILDREN: *3*
AGES: *10, 8 and 4 years*
WORK TIME: *Early morning & evening*
NUMBER OF HRS/WEEK: *21*
STUDIO LOCATION: *Breakfast room*
TYPE OF ART: *Graphic art, illustration, photography, mixed media*
WEB SITE: *www.blu-bambu.com*

When Shannon was in art school and later when working as a corporate artist for a national restaurant chain, she did not envision her life as it is today. As a corporate artist, she traveled around America working on murals. Today, she has carved out a lifestyle that includes both art and children. Now, Shannon is at home every day, living and working and learning alongside her children. She spends her days homeschooling her three children and in the evenings works as a freelance graphic artist and illustrator, mixed-media artist and photographer. Most of her art supplies, tools, laptop and mixed-media materials are housed in the same area where her children store their schoolbooks. Her breakfast room and living room are a hive of scholastic and artistic activity. Every nook and cranny is devoted to school and art. You might think that her space would be chaotic, but with her diligence and proactive planning she keeps her home neat, organized and artful.

The Muchas' eclectic home contains Asian artwork, mixed-media pieces, antiques and unusual bits and pieces that Shannon and her husband, Marcus, a designer, have collected over the years. The interesting things that surround her act as a source of inspiration for Shannon. She is also motivated by looking at other artists' work online, in books and magazines, listening to music, going to museums, going for walks and being outside in her garden. She finds inspiration all around and has learned to see art in everyday life.

Shannon incorporates art into her children's education. Her kids study art and history chronologically. (Seeing how art has developed and how it has influenced the events of different time periods helps Shannon in her own work.) Outside of school hours, the Mucha children are always surrounded by art supplies and are influenced simply by the fact that their parents are usually involved in some sort of creative project nearby.

SHANNON'S ADVICE FOR MOTHERS WHO WANT TO DO ART:

"Commit to sitting down and doing something creative every day, even if it is only for twenty minutes. Do something, brainstorm, plan something, make a mark on the paper, see where it leads you. You'll be surprised how that discipline helps in getting inspired and motivated. Another thing is to stop while you still have ideas flowing. That will excite you and make you more likely to continue the discipline the next day."

Shannon strives to make her family her first priority. In order to run and maintain their full home and school life, Shannon creates schedules for the family to follow. The schedules cover school subjects, social outings, chores and extracurricular activities such as martial arts for Zeb, ballet for Hannah and Nomi and piano for all. Shannon finds time for art each day. She feels that setting time aside in advance for art helps her to begin creating as soon as the kids are occupied or in bed. Her schedule keeps her productive and prevents her wasting time on unnecessary things.

Shannon sees her art as a privilege she enjoys. Over the years she has found that being creative gives her more energy. Art is part of who she is. If she denies her commitment to making art, she can lose her sense of self or purpose. She needs her creative outlet to keep her life balanced. Art helps her to be a better home manager, mother and wife.

Motivation

Motivation is an essential ingredient to
making sure you get artwork done. As moms, our days fill up
with things that seem totally nonartistic. When we focus on daily
life and children—the guidance, discipline and choices—it can
prove difficult to see the art in life or to feel up to creating.

In this chapter you will find some simple planning tools and
tricks that can motivate you to do art even on the days you are
not feeling artistic. Once you find that motivation and get started
seeing life artfully or actually creating something, you will find that
you already have the ideas, energy and drive you need. Use this
hidden motivation to propel you toward the dream of a life full of
things handmade and artistic.

*"The essential first step to building a life in the arts is simply getting past
the obstacles that keep that initial brushstroke from ever reaching the canvas in
the first place. After that it's just a slow but cumulative process,
changing the world one artwork at a time."*

TED ORLAND

The Artistic Vision Statement and Goals Lists

The first motivational tools you can use to help you get going when you are not feeling creative or to keep you motivated over the long haul are an artistic vision statement and long- and short-term goals lists. Vision statements and goals lists work together. The vision statement sets the tone of who you are or are becoming. Goals lists help you to get there or become that person. So it is important to develop both simultaneously.

If you take the time to make a vision statement and goals and then reread them at the end of a busy workday, they can redirect your thoughts, moving them away from the trials of child rearing and onto the positive dimensions of your children's personalities, hopes and dreams, while rekindling the flames of your love for artistic pursuits. As you do the things on your long- and short-term lists and tick them off, you create a record of what you have accomplished. Your successes in turn can motivate you to keep working to build on your achievements. Your lists can also serve as a guide when deciding what to do—what class to sign up for, what sites to visit on the Web, what to do when you find yourself with a free hour and no children about. When we see too many possibilities they can deplete our resolve to act. Having a focused path makes it more likely that we will get some art done.

Create an Artistic Vision Statement

An artistic vision statement should reflect your personality, values and aspirations, outlining the big picture—the direction you want your art to take.

In order to create an artistic vision statement, think of how you want to live your life—of ideals for which to strive. Be honest, but idealistic. Think big. Think of things that would sound ridiculous if you said them out loud. You may not be the woman you describe in your vision statement every day, but you can strive to live that way. If you rehearse your vision long enough, one day you will wake up and find you have become that person!

Develop a Long-Term Goals List

Long-term goals indicate concrete objectives you want to accomplish over the next two to five years. To create a long-term goals list, take some time to envision big goals that are attainable given your gifts and abilities. Your list should reflect your innermost desires, not what you think others would like you to do, nor what you think would earn you the most money. You can leave some goals open-ended, but for some you'll need a time frame.

Make a Short-Term Goals List

While big long-term goals inspire you and give you an idea of your final destination, short-term goals act as a road map to help you get there. They include actions you can take in the next few months as steps to accomplishing your long-term goals.

Write a list of things you think you can really accomplish over the next few months. What things are vital to achieving your goals? What area of your art life needs extra work? It is best to include small chunks of a larger project. Give yourself permission to be realistic when choosing your short-term goals. Consider your other commitments—you may not have time to produce fifty-two collages a year or have print-worthy photos to sell on Etsy anytime soon. Perhaps consider creating one art piece per month, instead.

FIVE-YEAR VISION

If you start now and do as little as thirty minutes of art, photography or writing each day, it will add up. Think of yourself in five years—would it not be better to have worked a little every day on your art for those five years than have done nothing at all?

SAMPLE VISION STATEMENT

I am a creative woman in love with life. Life is beautiful. I own that beauty. I am creating a body of work that reflects who I am. I do this every day regardless of how I feel, how I compare to others, how I criticize myself. I am creating a body of work that captures my view of life and my children through poetry, photography and mixed media. I am innovative, imagining new and wonderful things. I honor God, my husband and my children with all I do, feel, think and say.

SAMPLE LONG-TERM GOALS

★ Take stunning photos of my children

★ Write a book of poetry in the next two years

★ Be published in an art magazine

★ Write an article for a national magazine

★ Get a degree in art

★ Develop an art workshop to teach at a retreat in the next three years

★ Become an art teacher at the local community college

★ Learn to quilt

★ Exhibit a photo or art piece in a local gallery

SAMPLE SHORT-TERM GOALS

★ Write one complete poem this month

★ Write for five minutes daily in my poetry journal

★ Take five decent photos of each of my children

★ Send in one magazine submission by the end of the year

★ Read five chapters of a photo how-to book

★ Get an application packet from an online or evening school

★ Design the outline for a workshop this month

★ Make one handmade gift this month

★ Start a blog next month

★ Make a list of blogging topics

★ Make five birthday cards

★ Buy flowers and sketch them

★ Attend a poetry reading

★ Go to the art museum

★ Do one craft with my kids each week

★ Subscribe to a craft magazine

★ Read one poem to a friend

Suggestions for Using Vision Statements and Goals Lists

★ Once you have written your artistic vision statement and goals lists, it is a good idea to post them where you can read them. You will enjoy these much more if you decorate them, so consider printing or writing them out on some decorative paper. You might wish to print the different lists on the same sheet or make a book devoted to them. Decorate with rubber stamps, paint and collage elements (see Week 4 of the Workshop, page 82).

★ Keep your vision statement and lists beside the computer, pinned where you can see them from your craft table, by the bathroom mirror or glue them into an art journal. Move the lists weekly—after a few days the lists can become invisible to you and thus lose their power to motivate.

★ Revisit and rehearse the content of your lists weekly.

★ Revise your lists every three to six months. Your goals are not set in stone. As new ideas come to mind or you read about an art form that excites you, it is okay to follow that urge.

Accountability

The next tool you can use to keep your creative focus fixed and your motivation high is accountability. Accountability involves having someone to answer to—someone outside yourself whom you trust and respect, someone who knows your goals and will remind you of them, keeping you organized and on track. You may have a friend and fellow mom who is interested in art who can serve as an accountability partner. Share ideas and vision statements. Check in with each other via phone, e-mail or even at a regularly scheduled play date or lunch.

An older child or teen or even your husband could be your accountability partner. Tell them your vision and goals and recruit them to gently remind you of them or to ask you how your art is going.

Similarly, online groups can offer a form of accountability. By signing up for a group or online art challenge, you not only meet other creative folks but also find something to work toward together.

Blogging can also keep you accountable. You become responsible to your readership (however small) to produce something worth viewing. Telling the world you are creating can be a scary thing to do, but it can also motivate you to live up to the vision you cast!

Consider submitting to magazines or online challenges or competitions. Check to see what the deadlines and themes are and find out the guidelines and parameters for submission. Once that goal is set and you know when the art is due, use your weekly creative time to complete the submission.

ROUND-ROBIN COLLABORATION

These books were made in a round-robin collaboration. One artist, Mendy Mitrani, invited a group of friends—myself, Carrie Harney, Sarah Keith and Cindy Mayfield—to take part in this project. Mendy, as host, formed the guidelines and contact list for the collaboration. The goal was to create altered books made by Texas artists, just for fun. Each artist started her book by decorating the cover and some pages in an alterable book. She mailed it to the next person on the list. Each participant then decorated one spread in each of the books she received in the mail and then sent it along to the next person and so on until each book was filled with collages and made its way back to the original owner.

Ritual

You can use rituals to trick yourself into doing art. Even if you feel totally spent at the end of the day, you can override the feeling with repetitive actions that lead you into art mode. Rituals are different for each person and you can develop them over time. As you work, become conscious of the little patterns of behavior that you do almost without thinking. Next time you find yourself in a tired slump, act out one of your rituals. Pretty soon you will be stamping or sewing or writing! Identify your rituals by considering each of the five senses:

Sound

Music can connect with parts of your mind or memory associated with creativity, beauty or inspiration. Whatever music you like to listen to as you create, turn it on, turn it up and let it carry you away. On the other hand, you may require silence or the whir of a fan or the hum of talk radio to get creating. Just identify what works and submerge yourself in it.

Taste

Perhaps you like to drink tea or soda using a special glass when creating. Or perhaps food gets you going. If you enjoy eating a bowl of ice cream or chocolate and it is art night, treat yourself.

Touch

Tidying up your art supplies can leave your mind free to wander to creative thoughts. The feel of oil pastels in your fingers or fabric on your skin may make you want to create. Sometimes exercising before you get creating can help. Exercising while listening to poetry on CD or watching a movie or even an art how-to DVD can help you focus on art, stimulating your mind while preparing your body for action and relieving stress.

Smell

Light a candle, burn some incense, put oils on your skin—whatever puts you in the art zone.

Sight

Consider hanging artwork that inspires you around your art space. Get a notice board and pin up images or words. Hang something you made and let the memory of making it as well as the images and concepts guide your current creativity. You can find motivation online or in the pages of magazines and books. You may feel sometimes that you are wasting precious art time when you peruse art blogs or sit reading magazines or books, but they stimulate ideas and provide raw material for your own artwork.

ANTI-RITUAL

Sometimes the creative mind needs change in order to flourish. Change your perspective; tackle a problem from a new angle; move your craft table to a new spot; go somewhere you have been meaning to go. Break the patterns. Create new ones. Enjoy the finding. Be crazy and spontaneous for at least one day. See the comfort and loveliness of your life and tell yourself you will be back, but for today you are trying something new. From this fresh perspective you may see the possibilities that are out there. Try it all on for size. Some days you will work best with familiar rituals. Other days new patterns may prove essential to creative revival.

Artist Spotlight
Corey Moortgat

NUMBER OF CHILDREN: *3*
AGES: *4, 3 and 1 years*
WORK TIME: *During children's afternoon naps and evening*
NUMBER OF HRS/WEEK: *10–20*
STUDIO LOCATION: *Sun porch off the kitchen*
TYPE OF ART: *Mixed media*
WEB SITE: *www.coreymoortgat.blogspot.com*

For Corey Moortgat, stay-at-home mom and author of the book *The Art of Personal Imagery,* art holds an extremely important place in her life as both an individual and a mother. It is her passion and chosen identity. Much of her artwork centers on motherhood and love for her family. She creates art as a visual representation of how much she loves her life and children.

Corey loves to be submerged in her own visionary world. She fills her home with artwork, both her own and that of others. The art inspires her to keep on creating, even when all she wants to do is veg out on the sofa and watch television.

Having her own studio space is an important get-going factor in Corey's life. Her husband turned the dining room into her art studio and created a doorway that opens into their family room. It works very well, as she is right off the room where her kids spend most of their time. When they play in the other room she can easily keep an eye on them while she creates.

While fairly small, Corey's studio is super functional. She has three bookcases in which she keeps all of her supplies. Most items fit in baskets or behind cabinet doors, so the room still looks attractive—an important aspect, since everything is visible from the family room. She keeps artwork and scrapbook papers in some large, flat

COREY'S ADVICE FOR MOTHERS WHO WANT TO DO ART: My biggest advice would be to get your kids on a nap/rest schedule that allows you to have some time to yourself each day. Nap time is when I do all my crafting, and even once my kids outgrow naps, I plan to still have "quiet time" in their rooms so that Mommy has some alone time every day!

drawers, and a U-shaped table fits among the bookcases. Corey keeps her sewing machine on one side of the table, and she works on the other side.

Corey has put much work into decorating her studio so it reflects her life and vision. It is full of girly, artsy things that don't fit as well in the other parts of the house that she shares with two little men and a husband as well as her baby girl. Corey's collections—vintage porcelain planters, head vases, doll furniture, paper dolls, artwork and other things that inspire her—cover every available space in her studio, so when she steps into it they always get her in the mood to create. Once she is in her studio, things start to flow, and she looks forward to a feeling of satisfaction in completing something.

Corey believes that having "just me time" during the day is essential to being a good mother and simply a happy person. For Corey, who has three young children, nap time is a saving

grace. Virtually all the artwork she does gets done during nap time—no cleaning, no chores, nothing except doing what she wants to do. Sometimes this may mean that the house isn't as clean as she may like, but she considers it a necessary sacrifice for sanity. Corey muses, "As long as the necessities are covered, does it really matter if I mop the kitchen floor today? It's only going to get dirty again by tomorrow!"

Corey's dream for her kids is that they will naturally desire creativity since they are surrounded by it in their daily lives and see their mother always engaged in art. The art Corey makes is about and for them, so she hopes that this will encourage them in their own love for the artistic life. She looks forward to the day when they are a little older and can do more art projects together with her.

Sweet

heartlight

my words touch the face of this child
written for her, day in day out
so she remembers the stories
that brought her here:

dream. create. present.

these are the days

To

strive

learn

dream

give

create

pray

Planning

Even if you feel motivated to do art, you may struggle to find the space in your schedule for creating. That is understandable given the hundreds of things that compete for your attention on any given day. But if you take an honest look at your schedule, you will probably find that some of the things you spend time on are not vital to either your mothering or your artistic goals.

This chapter challenges you to look at your life and recognize activities that you could do without, thus freeing up time for art. Making art a priority will help you to order your days and find the time to create in and around your motherly duties and activities.

"Good plans shape good decisions. That's why good planning helps to make elusive dreams come true."

LESTER R. BITTEL, *The Nine Master Keys of Management*

Creating Time

Are you feeling overwhelmed by all the possible art-related activities that clamor to be part of your week? Are you wondering where you could possibly find the time for even the briefest activity? Let's look at some practical, commonsense ways that we can reclaim and reorganize our time.

Time Stealers

Often time is wasted without us being cognizant of it. You may need to identify and trim some nonessential activities or habits from your life.

Nonpriority Activities

Consider limiting the following activities:
* Television
* Unfocused Internet surfing
* Inefficient or excessive house maintenance
* Non art-related hobbies
* Negative, unproductive or draining relationships
* Excessive shopping

Neglecting Family

Don't neglect your children in order to make it to the craft table. Neglected children act up in order to get your attention. Dealing with issues that arise as a result of your inattention zaps your time and energy.

Get your priorities in line with your goal to be an actively artistic mother. Take back those hours and give them to the artist in you.

Time Savers

Sometimes it takes a little time and energy to save time. By taking some simple actions, in the long run, your efficiency will increase and you will save time.

Keep an Ideas File

Dedicate a journal or notebook to jotting down creative ideas. Keep it handy and accessible so you don't lose good ideas.

Leave Work Out

Don't completely finish an art project on a given day. Leave something undone—an easy task that begs you to come make art the next day.

Get Organized

* Wash your brushes and straighten your work space each night so you can slip into your work easily the next time.

* Pack your camera or notebook in your diaper bag or purse the night before you go somewhere.
* Wear an apron with pockets for a pen and notebook or slips of paper to jot notes on.

Day Planning

In order to add art into your schedule you have to make a plan. Consider what else you have to do each day and plan an hour or so of art accordingly. Organization in the rest of your life is a big plus for achieving in the art world. Put some time into making sure that you are on top of your household chores and duties, as well as friendships and correspondences. That way you will feel freer to include art in your life.

Time Finders

Once you resolve not to waste time on too many nonartistic pursuits, you can begin to focus on finding extra time in the day to do the little steps that make up an artistic life.

In-Between Moments

* Keep a craft, poetry or photo how-to book in the bathroom.
* Get into the habit of bringing an inspiring book or your poetry journal in your diaper bag or purse. When in the waiting rooms of life— ballet, doctor, karate—you can read or write.
* During your lunch hour, when quietly nursing or feeding your baby, or when the kids are napping or at school, take a moment to plan a project, paint a background or write a few lines— something small and easy.

* Load your iPod with your art music selection or poetry. Listen to it during the day as you go about your daily activities. This will help remind you of the creative aspects of your life.

Plan Ahead

Look ahead in your family calendar to see what activities are on the horizon. Perhaps your kids are going to be at their grandparents' or camp for a few days or are going on a sleepover. Decide to get some art done when they are gone. Don't fritter away that precious time.

Natural Rhythms

Are you a morning or evening person? If morning, consider getting up a little earlier to complete a specific item on your art to-do list. If evening, get your evening chores out of the way and stay up an extra thirty minutes.

Include Your Children

Include your children in your art time. Tell them about your projects— how important art is to Mommy. Create an art space for them and help them make their very own art box. It will be hard to concentrate over the chatter and requests for help with scissors, but perhaps you can get one step of a project done while they create.

Ask for Help

Don't feel like a failure if you ask for help with the house and kids so you can find time in your schedule for your art. You can pay someone to clean your house or get a baby-sitter once in a while. Perhaps your husband or mother could take the kids to the park or out for a meal once a week so you can have uninterrupted time to work on a project.

Creating Space

In order to make time for art it is important to have an art table, desk or craft room. It does not need to be huge or fabulous at the start, but it needs to be functional. Having a dedicated, well-designed art space makes it a lot easier to turn up to work. If you have to get your supplies out every time you sit down to create, not only does that take up your time, but it sets the bar higher for your motivation to get to work.

When you have your space set up, consider decorating it over time with as much care as you would your living room. When you go there you want to feel comfortable and inspired. As you work in your space and hang up your artwork it will become beautiful. Decorate with things that say, "This is my creative room, this is me." Having an art space reminds us and our immediate family that art is important. Children can learn to respect Mommy's space, art supplies and art time. Our spouses can know the value of art to our lives and assist us in making time for art in the family schedule. The space dedicated to our art serves as a visual reminder and strengthens our commitment to a creative life.

Here are some things to consider when setting up your craft space:

* Choose a space that is not disruptive to the rest of your family. Try to keep your space contained and organized so it doesn't impinge on their activities. Conversely, you will want to be able to leave unfinished artwork and necessary tools out without being disturbed by others. Consider niches in your home like closets, unused formal dining rooms or garages that you could turn into work spaces. I craft in what was once a breakfast room (pictured above). Our family now eats all meals in the formal dining room instead.

* For mixed-media art you may need a few different surfaces. If you paint or use glue you will need a surface that you don't mind getting messy, or at least one you can cover with newspaper. For cutting or rubber stamping you will need a flat surface.

* Arrange shelving for your art supplies and books within easy reach of your work space. Store things you use infrequently on higher shelves or in closets.

* For photography, you will need a place to store your camera safely. Consider purchasing a lined basket to house all your extra lenses, batteries, computer wires and other accessories.

* Consider investing in an ergonomic computer table and adjustable chair. You will probably spend a significant amount of time at your computer processing digital photos, checking art Web sites and blogs, revising your poetry or completing other such lengthy tasks. To ensure that you don't get back, arm or finger pain, pay attention to the height of your desk and the position of your keyboard. As a rule of thumb, a desk should be about 30" (76cm) off the floor and your computer approximately 20" (51cm) from the eye.

* You will need access to electrical power for your heat tool, drill and other tools. For your computer, printer, external hard drive or recharging your camera batteries, a surge protector is important.

* Your space should have adequate lighting. In the daytime, natural light is best. If you have a room that is dark or work in the evening, you will need both ambient and spot lighting. You may want to invest in some true light lightbulbs.

The Art Action Plan

Being conscious of what you want to achieve in a day is vital to living a creative life. An art action plan is a list of things that you would like to accomplish during the week, including things that are doable given your available tools and supplies and the time that you have to devote to art. You may only have an hour or less a day, but you can still learn to use that time effectively. Write your list on loose notepaper pinned to your fridge, in your day planner or on a computer calendar. Alternatively, you could create a blank document to reproduce each week on decorated paper (see Week 1, pages 68–71, for details).

When you start out, try committing to an hour of art a day. If you think you can get two things done in sixty minutes, for each day pick two things to put on your weekly action plan. For example:

* Monday—Read a poem, write ten lines

* Tuesday—Listen to an audio poem on the Internet, revise a poem

* Wednesday—Read a poem, write six observations in your journal

Take time at the end or beginning of the week to make a plan for the coming week. Print a blank copy of the plan (or get out your calendar or planner) and fill in things to accomplish on each day. As with your vision statement and goals lists, leave your art action plan visible beside your computer or on the kitchen counter all week and refer to it often. Each morning at breakfast, review the list of things to do that day. Fit the art action items into your household or work schedule. Then as you complete a task, mark it off your list.

The key to making weekly action plans work is flexibility. If some days you can't do an action item on your list, that is okay. Try to squeeze it in another time or give yourself permission to skip it (but not too often). Some days you may feel the muse taking you further on a project than you intended, or you have more time because the kids are being super cooperative and are in bed early or are at a friend's house—great, go with it! You don't want your list to become an idol that controls and depresses you. It should act as a guide to help you get art done. You run the risk of burning out your artistic motivation if you have to strain to meet your own expectations. Be gentle with yourself.

There is a true ebb and flow to life. When making a plan for your art you must factor in the realistic ups and downs. There are legitimate times when you are not going to be creative—during times of family vacation, holidays or illness, for instance. At other times, your intensity will simply be lower. On those days, do the minimum amount of art. When planning your schedule, plan some days with a lighter workload. Even taking one small step toward your big art goals is better than nothing. And remember, sometimes you will actually need to give yourself a break. It is okay to sit down, watch a movie, go out for coffee with a friend, cuddle with your kids or have a date night. You deserve a break. When you take a break, enjoy it.

Of course, it is important to learn to recognize habitual down behaviors and to use your action plans to blast on through. You want to push yourself—just not to the point of burnout.

SAMPLE ACTIONS

* Visit photo blogs

* Take at least ten photos

* Choose photos for walls, get them printed

* Organize photos by theme

* Combine poems and photos

* Listen to a poem online or on CD

* Write ten lines of a poem

* Revise one poem

* Make six real-life observations

* Read a craft book

* Check five art blogs

* Plan magazine submission art

* Make a background page

* Make one collage bookmark

* Plan art projects for the month

* Work on a project from a book or magazine

* Tidy the craft table

* Plan art for the house

* Read your vision statement

* Read your long-term goals list

* Make an art action plan

NUMBER OF CHILDREN: *3*
AGES: *17, 15 and 11 years*
WORK TIME: *Morning and late night*
NUMBER OF HRS/WEEK: *20*
STUDIO LOCATION: *Attic*
TYPE OF ART: *Mixed media*
WEB SITE: *www.rebeccasower.typepad.com*

Artist Spotlight
Rebecca Sower

When Rebecca Sower is not using her spare time to work on her mixed-media art, she is working on her home hobby farm. How does she do it all? The answer is priorities. Rebecca has always put her family at the top of her priority list. When her children were younger, and now when they are home from school, she spends less time in her studio and remains content to work on small projects or sketch out ideas that she can expand upon later.

Rebecca makes the most of every day by meticulously scheduling time to work in her art studio and on her farm, and by cutting things out of her life that are not high on her priority list. For example, she does not spend time watching television, as she believes, "Each moment of our lives is a moment we'll never get back. Time spent with family and art will always be well spent."

Over the years, Rebecca's art has become a part of who she is. She likens art to a golden thread that runs through her life—always there at some level, though sometimes more visible, sometimes less so. She believes that she is a better wife and mother because of the time she devotes to nurturing her creativity.

To assist her, Rebecca's husband built her a large craft table tall enough for her to stand at as she works. Her studio is located in the attic and is far from orderly and clean. Rather, her creative space contains a wonderful and inspirational hodgepodge of all kinds of findings, fabrics, paints and

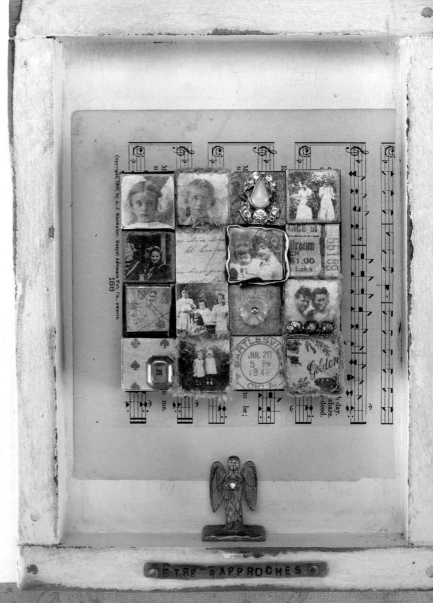

pieces. Being surrounded by her own art and work done by other artists' hands inspires Rebecca to create. She finds that buying a piece created by another artist brings art and inspiration into her life, especially during those times when she is unable to schedule studio time or feels artistically frustrated.

Rebecca also finds motivation in maintaining her art blog. Her weekly commitment to posting thoughts, musings, photographs and art images that encourage her readers to live creatively in turn motivates Rebecca to stay focused on art. Blogging is a sweet, steady form of accountability that assures she practices what she preaches.

Rebecca's art-time ritual starts with a trip to her coffeemaker for a fresh, hot cup of coffee. She likes to play all sorts of music as she works, letting her mood determine the genre. As the coffee aroma and the inspirational sounds fill the room, she creates her beautiful vintage layered mixed-media pieces that reflect her love of family, home and garden.

REBECCA'S ADVICE FOR YOUNG MOTHERS WHO WANT TO DO ART:

"My biggest piece of advice would be not to care what the neighbors think! Pull back from the cycle of trying to keep up with them by worrying about having a nice lawn, spotless home, over-the-top, latest-style clothes or gadgets. Don't try to impress people; it consumes a huge amount of time (and money) and often is not even serving yourself or your family. Constantly ask yourself why you're doing what you're doing. If you aren't satisfied with the real reasons, consider cutting it from your life. I think we all have plenty of areas where we can reclaim time."

Lily Kate

TREASURE

Media

In this chapter we will look at some basic tools, techniques and ideas in the disciplines of photography, poetry and mixed media/collage. Of course, you can enjoy each of these art forms individually, but I hope you will integrate them to create mixed-media work that has your images and your words. These are essentially the tools you will need to complete the projects in the Workshop section of this book starting on page 64. One of the goals of this book is to help you actually complete the workshop projects. To this end I have tried to keep the tools and techniques required to a minimum.

"A musician must make music, an artist must paint, a poet must write, if he is to be ultimately at peace with himself. What one can be, one must be."

ABRAHAM MASLOW

Photography

Photography is a wonderful life-recording tool. A photo captures life as it really is, then through simple processing you can elevate and beautify that reality. What you choose to shoot with your camera tells your personal story. Your choices speak volumes about how you see the world.

Even if you don't desire to learn how to take professional photographs, if you train yourself to take the time to photograph your life and your kids, you will be glad in the future that you did. Precious memories will come tumbling out with each image.

Whether you take pictures of your children, life events or the things you own, some simple tools and techniques can help you take better photos. The photos you take can then be used in your mixed-media work, adding layers of *you* to your artwork.

Top: Low f-stop (F-2);
Bottom: High f-stop (F-22)

A Beginner's Guide to the Digital Camera

Left: Low ISO (100) in bright light; Right: High ISO (1600) in low light

While there are wonderful cameras that use film, for the purposes of this book we will focus on digital cameras. The two main types of digital cameras on the market right now are point-and-shoot cameras and single-lens reflex (SLR) cameras. Point-and-shoots in general are designed so you can snap photos quickly with little technical know-how. They are small enough to carry everywhere and simple enough to use without much creative stress. However, in the end they limit you in what you can achieve in terms of quality.

SLR cameras are more complicated. Together with the many features and controls, the interchangeable lenses give you more control, but this added control comes at a price. To use an SLR successfully you must know about the camera's features and the camera modes or automatic settings. Here are some of the most common options:

ISO

A digital camera operates by letting light into a recording sensor. The ISO function sets the sensitivity of the image sensor to light—the higher the ISO, the more sensitive. If you are in a place with low light you will need a high ISO (800 or 1600). If you are in a bright place you will need a low ISO (100 or 200). If you use a high ISO, the resulting photos will appear softer and more grainy; a low ISO produces sharper photos.

Aperture and DOF

The aperture of a camera is the hole that allows light into the camera to record the image. Changing the aperture adjusts the volume of light getting to the sensor. The aperture acts like the iris of your eye. In bright light the iris narrows so less light gets in, while in low light the iris opens to allow the eye to see better. The size of the aperture is calculated in f-stops. The smaller the f-stop, the more light will pass into the sensor.

The aperture also controls the camera's depth of field (DOF). If you want to focus on a subject in the foreground while leaving the background out of focus, lower the f-stop (e.g., to f-2). Conversely, if you want the subject and the background to be equally sharp, choose a higher f-stop (e.g., f-16 or f-22).

Shutter Speed

Shutter speed indicates the length of time the shutter opens to let light into the camera's sensor. It is measured in seconds and fractions of seconds. The smaller the number, the faster the shutter speed (e.g., 1/1000 sec is faster than ½ sec). Faster shutter speeds generally produce sharper images, but sharpness also depends on the relationship between the ISO and aperture.

Modes

Digital cameras can have a number of modes or types of automation. In automatic mode the camera adjusts everything for you. It assesses the available light and adjusts the aperture, shutter speed and ISO automatically. On the other extreme is the manual mode. In manual, everything is adjustable. While the manual mode (not available on most point-and-shoots) gives you flexibility and control over your image, to use this mode you must really know how to adjust your aperture, ISO and other variables.

In between automatic and manual are a few other options. The different modes are designed to help you tell your camera what type of shot you plan to take. These might include portrait, macro (for close-up pictures), landscape and night modes. Again, these modes will help you get a good shot if you know in advance what you want and remember to adjust the camera to the desired mode.

There may also be some semiautomatic modes on your camera. Aperture priority mode (AV) allows you to manually adjust the aperture while the camera does the rest (shutter speed, ISO, white balance). Shutter speed mode (TV) lets you adjust the shutter speed while the camera adjusts the rest. Program mode (P) allows you to adjust the ISO while the camera adjusts the aperture and

shutter speed automatically. For a mom taking photos of children and just learning to use the camera, it is best to use the P (program) mode. It is fairly easy to judge the ISO needed for the environment and to switch that one function as needed as opposed to worrying about aperture and shutter speed.

Camera Shake

Most photographers hold the camera in two hands to get a shot. When you press the button on a camera to take a picture, a slight movement necessarily occurs. This camera shake produces images that are not totally crisp. If the shutter speed is slow (e.g., at 1/50) the shutter remains open longer and tiny camera movements are even more likely to show up.

If you want to improve the sharpness of your shot, you can take a number of actions. You can work to improve the lighting—turn on room lights, move to a window or resort to using the flash. You can try to steady your hands by pressing your elbows into your sides or find something to lean your elbows on, such as a fence, table or your car. You can use a tripod and a remote shutter release trigger that ensures that your

wobbly hands never touch your equipment. But before taking these steps, consider leaving the perfectly sharp photos to the professionals. The beauty in your world is not always crystal clear and perfect. Some of my favorite photographs are the blurry, caught-moment shots.

Shooting

When just about to shoot, look through the viewfinder and decide on the main subject. Check that your subject is in focus by pressing the shutter release button half way—the camera detects the closest image and locks the focus on that focal length. Look for a good composition (see pages 38–39). Check the background. If you see distracting objects, move your camera or yourself and repeat the process. Even if the shot is not perfect, take it anyhow. Shots can be improved in postprocessing.

Remember to carry your camera with you everywhere, and take, take and take photos. Even if you are not feeling artistic, you never know when the perfect lighting or outfit will present itself. Be ready.

Left: Slow shutter speed (1/6); Right: Faster shutter speed (1/320)

Try changing the angle of your camera for a more interesting composition.

Composing a Photo

While taking photos, it is important to start to think of how a shot is composed. Composition involves the design or arrangement of the elements in an art piece. Good composition directs attention to the main subject of the photograph. Some basic principles of composition can guide you when imagining the photos you want to take, when actually taking them or when sifting through them to process for printing or use in mixed-media work. Let's look at some tools that can help you discover different compositional designs.

Camera Angle

Changing the angle of your camera helps you find interesting shots. If you stand on one spot and point your camera straight, then up in the air, looking down and at every degree in between, you will see a variety of possible shots. If you are shooting a particular object or even your child, you don't have to just take shots at eye level. Don't be afraid to get on your knees or climb up on the kitchen counter. When photographing your kids it is good to sometimes get on their level—to see the world from their

point of view and capture their faces straight on. Let the movement wake your creative juices.

Lighting

In the absence of expensive lighting equipment, the best lighting for taking photos of people is natural light. If taking pictures indoors, seek out a spot near a window for the best results. If a room is lit by a regular tungsten lightbulb (which has an orange tint) or fluorescent light (which has a greenish tint), adjust the white balance accord-

ingly. The camera will adjust for the color of the light, removing the tints so you have less to process later.

Outdoors, the best times to shoot are before 11 A.M. and after 3 P.M. Avoid harsh sun, as white objects may become overexposed and portrait subjects may have to squint. Look for even shade. People debate whether to use the built-in flash on digital cameras or not. The flash tends to flatten out a person's features and reflect off shiny surfaces, making the colors look unnatural. However, in some cases you will have to use the flash—for instance if you are in a low-light area and want a sharp image. If you are in low light, try raising the ISO before you decide to turn on the flash.

Backgrounds

Don't just look at the main subject. Consider the background of the shot, too. Check for distracting objects or lines. If something distracts from the subject of the photo, correct it before

These photos demonstrate the difference between shooting with the flash on and off. The photo on the left is taken with the flash. The flash was turned off for the photo on the right.

In the shot on the left, there is only one focal image. In the image on the right, the child on the left acts as the secondary image in the photo.

you shoot by moving to a new position, changing your camera angle, moving your subject to a new spot or changing to AV mode and setting the aperture to a smaller number to blur the background.

Focal and Secondary Images

The focal image is the primary image in a photograph that serves as the subject of the composition. The secondary image enhances or describes the focal image further, even by way of contrast. Avoid having too many strong secondary images as the clutter may confuse the eye and reduce the impact of the photo.

Symmetry and Asymmetry

One way to compose photographs is with a symmetrical design, where the focal image is front and center. This kind of design, in general, feels balanced and calming but also formal and non-dramatic. Asymmetrical designs have an off-center focal image, either to the left or the right, top or bottom of the picture. Asymmetrical designs can feel dynamic and spontaneous.

Rule of Thirds

If you lay a tic-tac-toe grid over a photo, it breaks the picture up into thirds. The places where the vertical and horizontal lines meet are the strongest places for the image in an asymmetrical composition.

The action in this photo takes place in the left third of the photo.

Filling the Frame

Often when looking through the lens or viewfinder, our minds trick us into thinking we have a great composition when in reality there is too much going on. To overcome this, get closer to the subject by zooming in or physically moving closer before you shoot. At other times a photograph works best with a lot of blank or background space around the focal image. The space gives the subject importance and breathing room.

Texture

You can compose layouts around and incorporate different surface qualities. You may want to capture rough textures like dry leaves or the fabric of your child's dress, or perhaps you want to record the smoothness of your baby's skin.

Try capturing the texture of your life.

Line

When a composition has strong lines, the lines make a visual path that allows the eye to move across the page and between images. It is best to have one predominant line type or direction in a shot.

Color

Color is a powerful compositional tool. A photo composed of many different colors says something different than one with a limited or subdued color palette. Colors either draw attention to or distract from an image. Look for threads of color—different objects with similar colors—while composing a shot. Similar colors used repeatedly in a shot can accentuate a focal image. For example, if your child has green eyes, have her wear a green outfit or stand in front of lush foliage to bring out her eyes. If you are doing a portrait of your child and she is wearing pink, you may not want that bright yellow and green bike in the background because it could draw the viewer's eye away from the main subject.

DEMONSTRATION
Photo Processing

Most printers, cameras and computers come with basic photo-editing software. There are also more sophisticated programs available for purchase, such as Adobe Photoshop, Adobe Lightroom or Corel products. While it is beyond the scope of this book to show you how to use a specific program, as each photo-processing program is different, here are some general ways you can improve photos by processing.

A simple processing tool you can use is to sharpen the image. When you sharpen an image, you can make the subject clearer and more defined. You can only sharpen an image that is already fairly sharp. It is not a tool that can rescue a photo that is blurry or was taken with a high ISO, such as 1600. (I also removed a distracting element from this photo, and upped the exposure.)

Upping the exposure on your photo has a similar effect to widening the aperture or upping the ISO. The light colors will appear lighter without affecting the darks.

Desaturate or fade your color for what I call the "cool movie look."

Saturate or boost your color for a stronger, bolder look.

If you brighten the image it allows a blanket of lightness to cover the whole photo. Both the lights and darks are brightened. It makes the whole image softer and can be used to give it a vintage look.

You can improve your composition by using the crop tool (I also brightened and converted this image to black and white).

Changing the color on your photo can change the feel of a photo.

Antique

TAKE THE TIME

The most important part of postprocessing is actually taking the time to do it! Use moments normally not devoted to art, such as when you are watching a movie at home or waiting for dinner to cook, or take your laptop computer with you to your kid's sporting classes or events and take a few minutes to process photos there. Plan on uploading photos from your camera every few days and work on them in small batches. That way you will never get overwhelmed.

Play around with the features in your processing software; consider reading a manual that teaches what your processing program can do.

Sepia

Original

More Green, Less Blue

More Blue, Less Green

More Red

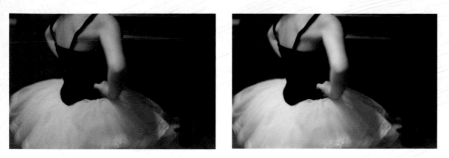

Converting to black and white is a great tool when there are too many colors in a shot, the colors are not attractive, you used a flash or you want to hone in on your subject. (Note: Typically you will need to adjust the contrast and/ or exposure levels when you convert to black and white.)

Unwanted background images can be removed with the cloning tool in Adobe Photoshop or Photoshop Elements.

Be subtle—a little processing goes a long way toward enhancing your photos.

DEMONSTRATION
Photo Distressing

Processing doesn't have to stop with your computer. This is a technique that I use often when I want to alter a professionally printed photo (that is, a photo not printed on a laser or ink-jet printer).

Materials List

Photo
Tray of hot water
Paper towels
Sandpaper
Acrylic paint
Oil pastels

1 To distress photos that are professionally printed, loosen the emulsion first by soaking the photo in hot water for a minute.

2 Pat dry with paper towels. Sandpaper around the central image—anything you don't want to show up. Start from the edges and work your way in toward the center.

3 Water down some acrylic paint and paint the sandpapered areas of your photo, working with different colors in small areas.

4 Mop up excess paint with a paper towel or rag. When your photo has dried completely, doodle over the painted areas with oil pastels.

WORKING WITH CHILDREN

Each child has a different personality. Some are camera shy, while others will strike a pose every time the camera comes out. In order to capture the unique aspects of your children, you need to have patience and realize that you will have to take lots of photos.

When you decide to do a photo shoot of your child, whether in a portrait session or in trying to capture her daily life or personality, ask permission first. Discuss what you want to do and why. This is especially important with older children. If they feel they have some control over the shoot, they may be more willing to play along.

Get your kids thinking about photography. Let them hold the camera and take a picture. Encourage them to suggest shots and listen to them when they do (even if it means photographing a beloved bear in odd places). If you always have your camera with you, they learn to expect it and even start seeing shots for you. Show them the photos when you upload them; point out why one photo is more successful than another; suggest how you could do things differently next time.

Make the photo shoot fun. Let your kids choose their outfits and props. Have them do things they usually do—things they can focus on so they forget to pose and smile for the camera. Expect movement and not perfection. Don't chastise your children for moving at the wrong moment and ruining the shot. Instead, move yourself, following your kids as they go about their business. Praise them for being good sports and helping Mom with her project.

When taking portraits, have your kids wear something simple—clothing that won't distract from your children's faces. Focus on filling the frame with their faces, with the primary focus on the eyes. If you are taking an impromptu portrait, take a quick minute to wipe their faces. Dirt can be difficult to remove in postprocessing.

Don't try to include too many things in the background. Move your child or yourself until you have a relatively clear background. However, if all else fails, you can crop or remove unwanted backgrounds with processing tools.

If photographing your children on any given day frustrates them, give it up. But there is no reason to end your photo shoot time. Train your camera on the details of your surroundings instead. Perhaps even coax your child into a better mood by talking to him about the other things you plan to shoot instead. Let him suggest objects or colors or angles to shoot. Let him see you are not upset with him. Try the kid photo shoot on another day.

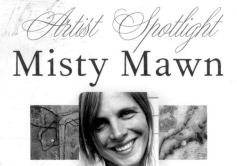

Artist Spotlight
Misty Mawn

NUMBER OF CHILDREN: *2*
AGES: *8 and 6 years*
WORK TIME: *Evening & night*
NUMBER OF HRS/WEEK: *28*
STUDIO LOCATION: *In-home studio*
TYPE OF ART: *Mixed media*
WEB SITE: *www.mistymawn.typepad.com*

Misty Mawn was born an artist. She never lacks motivation or artistic desire. She truly fits the definition of the artist we learned about in school: creative, free-spirited and unbound by the world. "If I had all the time in the world [to create], it still wouldn't be enough," Misty says.

Before she had her two children, Misty worked as a potter and mixed-media artist. Art completely filled her life. Now that she is a mother, she still feels that art is her life, but her children are now her first priority. If someone becomes sick or needs her, she puts time in the studio on hold.

When Misty's children were younger, she pushed art aside temporarily, recognizing that motherhood required her full attention. But Misty was comfortable with that season in her life, as somehow when her babies were little she did not crave art like she had before they were born. Being a mother of babies satisfied her to the fullest. Then slowly, as her babies became more self-sufficient and independent, she felt the desire to create art return to her.

Misty's creative space is usually a little disheveled. It becomes more so the longer she works on a piece. If you visited her today in her studio, you would know how hard at work she has been by how messy her studio appears!

Once she puts her children down for the evening, Misty makes her way to her art space. Music plays—anything from the moody Nina Simone, playful DeVotchKa, or the soothing sounds of the Clogs. Pieces from her favorite artists hang on the walls, all there to bring inspiration anytime she needs it. In addition, she surrounds herself with the work of her children—from paintings, to papier-mâché, to cities of blocks—all acting as visual stimulation and reminders of her motherhood.

Before she starts working, Misty spreads her collection of favorite papers out on the floor and sets all of her paints within reach. Her easel is loaded with work in progress, while more art pieces cover the table, and still others are scattered on the floor. Within this apparent chaos, Misty finds her artistic voice and creates her ethereal mixed-media paintings or processes her soulful photography.

Misty strongly encourages her children to do art alongside her and always provides pads of paper, crayons, markers and art projects to keep them interested. She is careful to never push them. If they do not feel like painting, she suggests something else that they might enjoy doing. Misty knows that when they are ready to create art, the space and supplies they need are there for them. Her children see their mom's commitment to living artfully. Her lifestyle teaches them how important it is to do what they love with their lives and to follow their own dreams. What a beautiful legacy!

MISTY'S ADVICE FOR MOTHERS WHO WANT TO DO ART:

"I think it just comes down to priorities. If you love creating art then you must find time to do so. If that means giving up a few hours of sleep at night, do it! The reward is worth it, even though it is not always easy finding that balance between motherhood and artist. Both are such fulfilling titles to have."

Poetry

You may have never written a poetic word. You may have written some angst-ridden lines when you were younger that on second reading sound overly emotional or clichéd. You may remember being bored in English class when you had to pick poems apart line by line in order to get a good grade, or you may imagine poets as people propped on stools late at night reading to tiny crowds. You may not even see the point to writing poetry or believe that you could ever write anything poetic. So why attempt it?

Poetry, like art, is not the exclusive domain of teachers, teenagers and turtlenecked café-lurking intellectuals. No! You can make poetry a part of your life, too. You can record the details of your world in poetic language. You can elevate this one life you have and enjoy viewing it on a new level. Once you begin to write you may choose to use poetic reflections in your mixed-media art or combine them with your photographs. Your poems will add another layer of authenticity to your artwork. Don't worry, you don't have to try to please the literary world, or even read your poems in public. Rather, you can learn how to record your motherhood and life vision in a poetic way, for yourself, your art and your family.

What follows is a very quick overview of how to get started writing poetry. You will have the chance to create poems for some of the projects in the Workshop section of this book. There you'll find prompts and challenges to help you get going.

A Beginner's Guide to Writing Poetry

Just like the other art forms, poetry takes time, thought and practice. The creation of poetry has three major components. It begins with reading and listening to other people's poetry, continues with writing and then revising your own words.

Read and Listen

In order to write decent poetry you need to fill your mind with poetic words and images. The best way to do this is to read the work of other poets. Reading poetry exposes you to the various forms and rhythms that will form a model of good poetry in your mind. If you make poetry reading and listening a goal and break it down into small steps, it is doable even with your busy Momma schedule. Commit to reading or listening to one poem per day or per week. Borrow or buy poetry books and poetry on CDs.

Poetry is not just the written word. It is designed to be spoken, too. Listening to a poet or actor read poetry is a very different experience from simply reading quietly to yourself. As you listen, the rhythm and melody of the words become apparent. How the poet reads the poem can alter the meaning of the words.

There are many types of poetry: confessional, descriptive, narrative, lyrical and free verse, to name a few. In more traditional poetry the poet relies on specific patterns, forms, syllable counts, line lengths, end rhymes and other boundaries. In free verse the poet largely makes his own rules and rhythms. To discern your tastes, read examples of the different types of poetry. A good anthology can give you a wide variety of poets and poems.

Some days, focus on reading for pleasure and entertainment. Other days, read to learn. Analyze what you like about a poem. If you feel drawn to a particular poet, buy a book of his or her poems. Look for themes in the book. Study the metaphors. Look at your life in light of the poet's worldview.

Write

Write. Daily. Uncritically. Record what you see in a notebook or poetry journal. Carry your poetry journal everywhere. Put it beside your bed, have it with you when doing mundane tasks. That way when ideas or lines come you will be ready. Even ten minutes a day of writing is better than nothing. Write five to ten new lines every other day. Don't expect brilliance today. Push through disappointment and keep writing.

When you feel you are ready to compose a poem, first think of a subject or story that you want to describe or tell. Then find the appropriate words and lines that will convey it.

FIND WORDS

★ Observe your world, the things your children say and do—and record the details. Take note of events and let the details show your life's purpose, vision and emotion. Be sensitive to your surroundings. You have a beautiful life. Your children are unique human beings—look beyond the trials they bring and see the details: the round cheeks, the clenched fists, the laughs, the gifts they bring from the garden, the smiles.

★ Look at your photographs or art. Make a list of words, sentences or feelings that come to mind. Make a list of potential themes.

★ When words, phrases or images come to mind, record them as is. Don't try to form them into a poem yet.

★ Think in terms of the concrete rather than the general. Record what you actually see and know. Play with word associations. Look for metaphors (a comparison of things or concepts that are seemingly unrelated) to describe your ideas without resorting to clichés. It is better to use images that show happiness, like blowing bubbles, girls giggling, drifting white clouds, than to say, "I am happy." Maintain balance in your use of feelings or emotions. Describe real-life people, places or things rather than talk about how you feel about them. Let the story reveal your feelings.

★ Make lists of words that rhyme and others that have slant rhymes (words that are partial or imperfect rhymes, e.g., fun/fan, shard/garb), assonance (a repeated vowel sound, e.g., loud/sound), alliteration (a repeated consonant sound, e.g., girl/grabbed/grapes).

★ Pick a theme, activity or idea and write lists of words or lines that it inspires.

FIND LINES

Try this freewriting exercise: Pick an activity, person, place, object or idea and write a list of words that it inspires. Now use some or all of those words in sentences. Make a story or a description that reflects your life. Try to write at least ten lines on the topic at one sitting. Don't worry if nothing poetic comes out—this is just to get you started. Record these budding poems in your poetry journal or type them into your computer. Remain uncritical. Put your lines away for a few days. Then you will be ready to revise what you wrote.

"By writing poetry, even those poems that fail and fail miserably, we honor and affirm life."

TED KOOSER, U.S. POET LAUREATE (2004–2006)

Bruises

The days are often overcast, the sun struggles to shine through the layers of fog and cloud that hover above our neighborhood.

Sitting on her butterfly chair on the porch thinking of her sister, she presses the purple spot on her arm, not yet healed.

It is hard to hear them bicker over toys, shove and push for dolls and plastic food, pull books not shared

someone eventually cries cradling an arm or head or toe. or heart. I scold and sooth over and over. And now my arms ache.

These days I'm often walking out on the stones, face to heaven looking to see if there is the slightest chance of rain.

Revise

Poetic words can flow easily, but often when we later read them and the passion has died down they can seem a little overdone, repetitive or even nonsensical. Through revision, you can make an adequate poem much better. Don't get too attached to the first version. You must be willing to put it away for a while knowing you will revise it. There are a number of methods you can use to help you revise a budding poem.

ASK QUESTIONS

As you reread your lines, ask yourself the following questions:

* Are there any unnecessary words or ideas? Be brutal and cut them.

* Are there clichés? Look for a new way of saying something obvious.

* Do you tell and not show? Find a concrete way to show how you feel instead of stating it.

* Are there too many weak verbs, such as "to have" or "to do"? Use a thesaurus to find active verbs.

* Could you use stronger words? Consult your word lists or a thesaurus.

* Are the images or metaphors muddled? Simplify. Don't try to be overly poetic.

* Are there too many generalities rather than concrete details?

* Does the poem reflect your reality? Are the words true to you?

* Does the poem feel authentic? If, for example, you are writing about the outdoors, does the poem make you smell the outdoors and hear the crunching of the leaves?

* Is the narrative interesting? Compelling? Going somewhere?

* Are the line lengths working? Rearrange the lines, making them longer or shorter.

COMBINE POEMS

Perhaps you have worked on a similar theme in two different poems. Try combining them to come up with a new whole. Cut out lines that don't work. Perhaps start an extra line file for lines you like, but that do not work in the current poem. Use them in later poems.

REVERSE THE POEM

Start with the last section and work backward. See if it becomes more dynamic or makes more sense or has a better rhythm that way.

CHANGE PERSPECTIVE

Consider the poem from the reader's point of view. Pick an audience. Would that person understand or enjoy what you are saying? What does this poem tell your reader about you? Think of the poem specifically from your child's point of view. What would you change? Can you see words or concepts that you need to remove to make it more child friendly?

REWRITE IN PROSE

Rewrite your poem in prose, explaining in longer form what you are saying. Can you see any unnecessary words or concepts? Does the poem need restructuring? What elements, although dear to you, are unnecessary to the story? What is missing? Now rewrite the prose as a poem.

MAKE COMPARISONS

Read your favorite poems by another poet and then read your poem. Can you hear any similarities in your rhythm or metaphors? Can you hear your voice yet? What can you change to make it yours?

REVISIT WORD PROMPTS

Go back over any word lists you have made. Look for words that stand out for use in the current poem.

LISTEN TO YOUR POEM

Once satisfied with your poem, you need to hear it. Read your poem out loud to yourself or a friend. Record yourself reading the poem and then listen to it. How is the rhythm? Are there any awkward words or sounds? Are there words that you could change to rhyme (direct or slant) or to have a similar vowel or consonant sound?

Your poetic eye and ear will eventually kick in and guide the changes you need to make. Put the poem away for a week. After that absence, apply another revision process. If you repeat this pattern over and over, one day you will reread your words and find that nothing seems out of place. Then you will know you are done.

"The best reason to write regularly, to keep working over drafts...
is that they give the breath of inspiration more of a chance to slip into our lungs."

JOHN DRURY, *Creating Poetry*

DEMONSTRATION
The Evolution of a Poem

I took this photo at the end of a party at a friend's house. As I thought about that day and the photo, I generated a list of words and phrases: vague, cold, bare, distant, little white cottage, children, absence, voices, play, drift, no one about, free, late afternoon sun, grill, sausage, memory, trees, light, white, colorless, sad, loss. Note that some of the words are concrete, some more abstract, but they are in no particular order. Next, with the photo still open on my computer, I composed the first draft of a poem:

I know a place
vague in everyone's memory
curling in the late afternoon light
into my camera,
my aperture perpetually open

the voices in books promised
a cottage, children,
a porch swing, an overhang
that protects from the rains

today, a slight cold is settling
on our playtime
soon we will drift back inside
for German sausage and cake.

I decided that I would prefer to end with something a little more abstract than cake, so I reversed the poem. In order for it to make sense, I had to remove some lines and words.

A slight cold settles
on our playtime
soon we will drift back inside
for German sausage and cake

voices in books that promised
a cottage, children,
a porch swing, an overhang
that protects from the rains

vague now, curling
in the late afternoon light
into my camera,
my aperture perpetually open.

Next I felt I wanted to: (1) add a direct rhyme: shake/cake, (2) change the phrase "voices in books that promised" to "voices that promised," because "voices" suggests a larger influence than merely "voices in books," (3) add more concrete images: bare arms, fingers, (4) add a simile: "like a vague memory I cannot shake," and

(5) give the poem a title that makes the whole poem a metaphor for sadness or loss or fading reality, because I could see a theme emerging.

Here is the final version. I feel it complements the photo well.

Late Afternoon

Soon I will drift back inside
for German sausage and cake

a slight cold has settled
on fallen leaves, bare arms, fingers
like a vague memory I cannot shake

voices that promised
a cottage, children,
a porch swing, an overhang
that protects from the rains

curling now,
in the late afternoon light
into my camera,
my aperture perpetually open.

Artist Spotlight
Susan Tuttle

NUMBER OF CHILDREN: *2*
AGES: *4 and 6 years*
WORK TIME: *Night*
NUMBER OF HRS/WEEK: *15*
STUDIO LOCATION: *Custom-built studio overlooking playroom*
TYPE OF ART: *Mixed media, digital art, photography, writing*
WEB SITE: *www.ilkasattic.com*

For Susan Tuttle, stay-at-home-mom and author of two books: *Exhibition 36: Mixed-Media Demonstrations + Explorations* and *Digital Expressions: Creating Digital Art With Adobe Photoshop Elements*, creating art is vital to her sense of well-being. She understands the importance of attending to and developing her creative spirit. She says, "When I am lost in the creative process I feel a sense of peace and freedom. It is crucial for me to nurture this aspect of myself, and in doing so I feel it makes me a better mother. I become more energized, alive and happy because I am honoring all the parts that make up who I am."

Susan finds the creative side of her brain is continually active—she churns out ideas all day long, especially when doing things like cleaning, laundry and other chores that never seem to go away. She keeps a few notebooks scattered throughout the house and one in her purse so she can capture those creative ideas whenever they come.

Not only does Susan attend to her own creative well-being by doing art, she shows her children what it means to embrace a passion. She hopes that through her example they can learn to do the same. She encourages her children to experiment with art on a daily basis. Susan keeps on hand a large basket filled with art supplies like crayons, colored pencils, markers, paints, glitter glue and playdough. The children have their own spiral-bound visual journals that they can create in any time they wish. She doesn't try to show her children a standard way to draw, but rather encourages them to draw things in the unique way they envision them. She often tries to make art right along next to them.

These sessions may last anywhere from five to thirty minutes, depending on the kids' interest levels at the time. Her daughter has a passion for drawing and painting and can create for long stints. Her son is more drawn to movement-based activities, so usually does not spend as much time making art as his sister.

When the weather is warm, Susan and her kids make art together outdoors on their deck. They have a glass-topped patio table that is perfect for making messes on since it makes for easy cleanup. The top part of their driveway is paved and makes the perfect surface not only for bike riding and ball bouncing, but for chalk drawing as well. Susan keeps a large bucket of sidewalk chalk just inside the garage. Her kids enjoy drawing faces, practicing letters and drawing lines and shapes. It's a great opportunity for Susan to practice some of her drawing skills in a fun, no-pressure setting.

Susan's studio is nestled in one corner of the playroom, separated from the play area by a half wall that she can easily see over. When her children grow older, are more self-sufficient and attend school, she will be able to get some art done during the day, but for now she is content working mainly in the evenings. She has made her creative space a welcoming haven for herself. The space is filled with things she loves: vintage books, found objects from her town dump, antiques, a vintage shelf that she painted aquamarine, her own art, artwork from some of her favorite artists and heartfelt creations from friends.

When the kids are in bed for the night she enjoys settling in for an evening of art by lighting a scented candle in her studio, sipping a glass of wine, listening to her iTunes playlist, raiding her secret candy stash, touching and handling her paintbrushes and smelling the scent of paint. Her space gets pretty messy, but one of the great benefits of having a creative space all to herself is that she can leave a work-in-progress spread out on her counter and return to it the next evening.

SUSAN'S ADVICE FOR MOTHERS WHO WANT TO DO ART:

"Weave artmaking into your daily life. Multitask—which shouldn't be a problem, as mothers are frequently quite good at that. Consider doing detail work or doodling in your journal with a gel pen while sitting next to the kids as they play in the bathtub, talking on the phone or as a big pot of soup simmers on the stove."

Mixed Media and Collage

In this section we will look at the tools used in the making of the mixed-media projects in this book. Mixed media is the combination of more than one art medium. A mixed-media artist uses various color tools—paints, pencils, inks and so on—as well as a variety of image types—photos, photocopies, stamped images, fabric images and so on—to create a single piece of art. You can create mixed-media artwork on any number of substrates—paper, canvas, fabric, cardboard, wood. This variety makes mixed media a versatile, accessible and exciting art form.

Since the focus of this book is on fitting art into your busy mom schedule, the supplies I have listed can all be purchased at local art and craft stores in your area or online.

A Beginner's Guide to Mixable Media

Awl

An awl is great for poking holes in cardboard, paper and beads. Awls are also great mark-making tools.

Cutting Tools

Have on hand large, small and decorative scissors. Use a dedicated scissors for fabric—cutting paper blunts the blades. Craft knives with replacement blades are cheap and easy to use. Paper cutters are useful for trimming large papers or for making accurate angles. They come in many different sizes. A self-healing cutting mat is a must for collage artists. It is marked with lines so you can line up papers when trimming.

Drill

A regular household drill with a $^1/_8$ (ISO 3.2mm) drill bit is essential for making holes in canvas or wood.

Eyelet Setting Tools

Finish off and strengthen holes in paper with eyelets. To finish off holes drilled in wood or canvas for hanging artwork, simply glue the eyelet in the hole.

Fixative/Sealer

Fixative is essential for sealing work with pastels or nonsolvent-based inked images.

Gel Medium

You can use gel medium as glue or for sealing artwork. It dries clear and functions as a fixative.

Gesso

Gesso is traditionally used for priming canvas to receive paint. Collage artists also use it for toning down work that is too bright and covering up mistakes. Apply gesso just as you would paint.

Glue

Liquid and spray glues are great for large surfaces. Acid-free tapes are dry and good for adhering photographs to paper. Stick glues are handy for both small and large areas.

Heat Gun

You'll need a craft heat gun when you want something to dry quickly.

Iron

You will need an iron any time you use cotton fabrics.

Paint

The paints used for the projects in this book are all acrylics. They come in hundreds of colors, dry fast and go on opaque or semitranslucent. You can apply paint full strength or watered down for different effects. You can easily cover up acrylic paint if you make a mistake. Avoid using paint straight out of the bottle. Mix it with other colors or tone it down with white.

Paint Application Tools

It is good to have a variety of paint-brushes on hand. Also, old credit cards or paint scrapers are a great way to drag color across a surface. Disposable painter's rags purchased at hardware stores are more absorbent than kitchen paper towels. They are great for wiping brushes, cleaning up spills and blending paint and oil pastels.

Paper Punches

Punches come in a wide variety of shapes, from basic circles to elaborate corners and images.

Pencils

Colored pencils are wonderful for filling in small areas with color. You can use lead pencils to add doodles or other details that give your work that artistic, handmade feel.

Rubber Stamps and Ink Pads

Inks come in pigment, dye and solvent form. Pigment ink is thicker and takes longer to dry. Solvent inks are permanent and can be used on almost any surface. They are great when you want to overpaint your image. Rubber stamps range from cute to artsy, focal images to background graphics, from words to letters, large to small.

Sandpaper

You can purchase sandpaper—used for distressing and altering surfaces, images and photos—from a hardware store. It comes in various grits, from fine to coarse. Sheets of sandpaper are more manageable if cut into small pieces.

Sewing Machine

Consider sewing paper and fabrics into your mixed-media work. Stitches and threads bring a lovely texture and handmade look to your work.

Steel Ruler

A steel ruler, especially one with padding on the back, is a good tool to use when cutting straight lines with a craft knife.

Water-Soluble Oil Pastels

Water-soluble oil pastels go on like regular oil pastels, but with a little water you can blend them to look more like paint. Pastels are messy, so remember to wash your hands after using them.

Building Your Art Stash

All of the projects in the Workshop section of this book require that you have a stash of papers ready to use. You will need papers to use as backgrounds to work on and images and lettering that serve as focal points for your art pieces.

Examples of items to include:

Magazines and Books

Old novels, children's books, music manuscripts, magazines and catalogs are great sources of words and images to alter and include in collages. Be a hoarder of images—you never know what will be useful for future projects.

Paper

Include scrapbook paper, recycled papers (junk mail, newspaper, tags, tickets), handmade papers, computer paper, watercolor paper. There are many different types of specialty printable papers available, such as iron-on fabric (silk, cotton, canvas), image-transfer paper, magnetized paper, shrink film and sticker paper. I recommend giving them all a try!

Photographs

As an alternative to getting your photos professionally printed, you can print them at home on your ink-jet printer on photo paper (matte or glossy) or regular computer paper. Every time you set up an 8½" × 11" (20cm × 28cm) document to print an image for an art piece, fill up the rest of the page with other images. Trim the extra images and add them to your stash.

Rub-Ons

You can transfer rub-ons to your artwork by placing the image or words face down and rubbing the back with a burnishing tool such as a bone folder or wooden craft stick.

Stickers

Scrapbook stores offer a wide range of image, word and letter stickers in many finishes, from paper to plastic, 2D to 3D.

Your Art

When you create a piece of art that you really like, scan it into your computer. Print it out, trim it and add it to your stash.

Choices in Creating a Mixed-Media Piece

There are a number of choices to face as you create a mixed-media art piece. You decide on the purpose of your piece. Is it to be a record? Is it to be decorative or functional or both? You choose the size of the piece and the substrate—canvas, paper, wood. You choose the focal image, color scheme, words, backgrounds and embellishments. To help you make these choices while imagining and researching, look at art magazines or books and see what is inspiring. As you envision your project, jot notes in a journal or on a scrap of paper; draw a quick doodle or sketch of the idea. Take time to observe real life. Look for connections between images and colors, metaphors, humor, wisdom. Play with different combinations in your mind and on paper. Be open, flexible, aware, explorative.

Subject Choice

Every artist at some point has to decide what vision to project, what subject to delve into artistically. While every part of life is open to interpretation, to me there is nothing quite as satisfying as painting a picture of the beautiful life I have as a mother. As moms we have the basic raw ingredients for our art right in our homes: the day-to-day, minute-by-minute ups and downs of raising children.

No one can attend to the details of your child's first haircut, favorite lunch or evening routine as you can. Your children are growing up right before you. There are stories that will later make sense in the big picture of who they become as adults, and there are stories that are also shaping the woman you will be when the one-on-one child rearing is over. As a mother, you can capture those stories and make art with them.

All of your art doesn't have to be a scrapbook of your life, but your art will feel more authentic when you study and reflect on things you know well. Let your life and surroundings be the jumping-off point for your art. Here are some places to start when looking for a subject for your art.

LIFE'S LITTLE DETAILS

You can train your eye to see the details of your life as special, unique and worthy of study. The following is a list of possible details you could photograph, write about or try to capture in paint and collage:

Daily life—Picked flowers, sippy cups, bottles, drinks, a favorite doll, trucks, block formations, lunch, bath toys, diaper bag, book piles, toy foods, kids' art, school bags, pencils and pens, art supplies, tea sets, berry pails, garden findings, gym equipment, makeup, cell phones

Body—Eyes, lips, smiling cheeks, wide-open-mouth laugh, pointing fingers, dirty hands, chocolate mouth, grumpy face, bare feet

Movement—Running, spinning, dancing, pointing toes, kicking a ball, throwing a fishing line, playing with the dog, climbing on Daddy, singing, accidents

Weather/Seasons—Lying in the sun, sunscreen, splashing at the beach, beach toys, name written in sand, sundresses, smelling flowers, windy days, playing in the leaves, in the rain, umbrellas, snow days, snowmen, hands holding a snowball, red cheeks, cold breath

LIFE'S SPECIAL MOMENTS

To create a mixed media collage that captures life's special moments you need to train your eye to pay attention to the details that surround the moment. Start collecting ticket stubs, brochures from events, magazines with relevant images, small tokens your children give you, pages torn from children's books and certificates. Make a note of colors, words and quotes that spark memories or emphasize lessons learned. Take photos that are both contextual and detailed. All of these things can be used in your mixed media work.

Here are some examples of events you may wish to record:

Outings—Zoo, trip to see relatives, going to the grocery store, visiting Daddy at work, play dates, sharing, off to school, going on an airplane, in the car, at the library

Big Events—Birthdays, baptisms, first day at school, competitions, graduations

Small Events—painting, time with friends, wearing a new outfit, building a fort, losing a tooth, reading, quiet time, building a block tower, giving gifts, siblings hugging, helping in the kitchen, smelling roses

LIFE'S INTANGIBLES

Sometimes when you photograph or write about your kids you will capture something more than just the facts. Art can depict the essence of a personality, emotion or concept. The following is a list of intangible ideas that you could focus your mixed-media art, photography and poetry on:

Emotions—happy, sad, grumpy, thoughtful, questioning, joyful, content, purposeful

Concepts—innocence, sweetness, togetherness, loneliness, calmness, loss, difficulty, childhood, marriage, motherhood

Color Scheme

Another choice made in the creation of a mixed-media piece is the color scheme. Here are some ideas to get you thinking about color choices:

★ Rummage through your images, backgrounds, old fabrics, magazines and craft paint bottles. Lay them out, grouping colors from the different color families until you find the perfect combination.

★ Listen to your feelings about color. Combining lots of odd colors together can feel crazy and fun or just plain confusing. Using colors from one family can feel harmonious and subtle but also boring. Let your personality show—what colors do you always fall back on? What colors make you feel good, uplifted, serene? Perhaps you need to throw in some dark colors to express rebellion or passion.

★ Use colors in the same family, then throw in a complementary color to draw the eye.

★ Make a commitment to a particular background, scrapbook paper or image and let it dictate your palette.

★ Limit your palette to four colors— one in each family, one blue, one green, one red, one yellow.

★ Consider the style and color of the room you will display the art in. If the art is for your son's red and brown room, you may narrow in on warm and neutral pallets.

★ Go against the grain. If making a Christmas gift or ornament, don't choose red or green. If your house is all beige, consider making art that screams—perhaps something yellow or purple.

★ Sometimes it works to choose colors you don't like. A color you don't like can cause you to disconnect from the work; this sense of disconnection frees you to make mistakes or go in an unexpected direction. It is fun to choose colors that typically don't go together, like turquoise and red, olive green and pink. Play with colors; break the sensible rules; throw random colors down and see what they show you.

★ Let the color palette of your favorite movie inspire you. Take note of scenes in which the colors seem to express that feeling you want. Similarly, steal color combos from art masters. Look at the work of your favorite painters and study how they combine colors.

★ Have your child pick out paints for you. See what crazy messes you can make. You can always tone it down with a wash of gesso!

Composing a Mixed-Media Piece

While the principles of composition in a mixed-media piece remain the same as for photographic composition (see pages 38–39), the actual act of composing is different because you use your hands, rather than just your eye, to manipulate the elements. You can take your time moving the images around and reworking the look until you find a composition that you feel is complete.

Here are some examples of composition in mixed-media layouts.

Today's Spills, *by Shelley Kommers, exemplifies the rule of thirds.*

believe

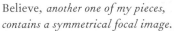

be•lieve (bĭ-lēv′) *v.* **1.** To accept as true or real **2.** To credit with veracity **3.** To expect or suppose

Believe, *another one of my pieces, contains a symmetrical focal image.*

Sweet

Sweet, *by yours truly, is an example of assymetrical composition.*

Look Up, *by Shelley Kommers, has a bird as a secondary image.*

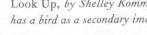

Mindy Mitrani's round robin book exhibits interesting texture.

MIXING MEDIA

When combining different art forms, you always have a chicken-or-egg conundrum: Do you choose the image first and then find the words, or write the words and then find or create images?

In practice, sometimes the image will lead to the words, other times the words will demand a particular color or shape to accompany them.

When combining images and words, try not to be too literal. You may lose the artistic impact and leave your audience with little interpretive room. For example, if you write about a sippy cup, avoid coupling the words with a picture of a sippy cup. However, there are two exceptions to this rule: One is if you are doing a handmade journal or scrapbook and the image is in a different part of the book; the other is if you are writing something to read to your child—often kids enjoy literal interpretations.

Mixing Poems With Photographs

★ You can write the poem first and then either plan out a photo shoot or just keep the poem in mind and look for shots, angles and focal images that complement the poem.

★ Use images that speak to you and then write a number of words that the images evoke. Write a list of words, ideas, feelings, colors, associations, even stories that the image prompts. Use those words as prompts for a new poem.

Using Poems in Mixed Media

★ Print a finished poem onto various papers: painted backgrounds, blank white paper, vellum, clear adhesive paper and so on. Keep a file of the poems. When you create mixed-media art, consider poems that would complement the theme or concept of the piece. Pay attention to the colors, images and themes that the poem evokes.

★ Use individual lines from your poems in your art, treating your poetry like a famous or inspiring quote.

Using Photos in Mixed Media

★ Pick out one of the colors in a photo to use in your collage or painting. Hint at it. Try to avoid being too matchy-matchy. If the photo is soft, then lean heavily on the gessoed, wispy look. If it is a bright, cheerful photo then look for bold backgrounds, stamps and paints.

★ Once you start a mixed-media piece, gather photos from your stash box. Lay them out with paint swatches, background papers and so on. See which image speaks loudest and go with it. Glue it down. If later you change your mind, you can always rip it off, cut it out or gesso or glue another image over it.

Background Papers

Here are some of the basic techniques I use over and over to create backgrounds for my mixed-media art. These are all demonstrated here on paper, but can be used on canvas, wood, cardboard or fabric with varying outcomes. You don't have to be a painter to create some interesting effects with paint and gesso. Just have a go and enjoy the act of creating!

Materials List

Gesso
Paper
Acrylic paint
Paint scraper or credit card
Water
Rag
Paintbrush

Paint Blending

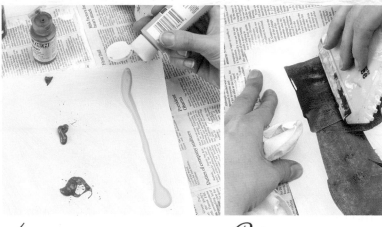

1 Start by applying drops of three different full-strength paints to a gessoed surface.

2 Use an old credit card or paint scraper and drag it through the paint.

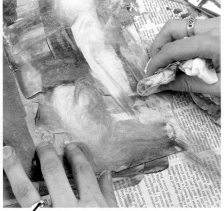

3 There is no need to clean the scraper between paints.

4 When the page is almost completely covered, add a few drops of water and switch to a rag. Using a circular rubbing motion, smooth and blend and remove some of the paint.

Monoprinting

1 Start by applying drops of paint on a half sheet of gessoed paper. Spread the paint around with a brush or rag.

2 Lay another piece of paper over it.

3 Rub or burnish the back and then peel apart. You will have 2 half sheets of textured paper.

4 Add a second color to the areas that are still unpainted and blend with a rag.

Toning It Back

1 If there is any excess paint on the paper or you want a more subtle color, drop some water on the paint and blot it off with a rag. Let the page dry.

2 Paint some gesso on the page over the current paint. Use the same rag to wipe and blend the gesso all over the surface.

Ellene McClay

NUMBER OF CHILDREN: *1*
AGE: *17 years*
WORK TIME: *Day*
NUMBER OF HRS/WEEK: *30*
STUDIO LOCATION: *Living room*
TYPE OF ART: *Mixed media, sewing, jewelry*
WEB SITE: *www.deciduous-soul.blogspot.com*

Ellene has always designed, made and improved things. She learned early in life to be resourceful and to think like an engineer to find new ways to make things work—whether it involved designing curtains or rearranging a space. When she was young, if Ellene liked a certain style of clothing and it wasn't in the family budget, she would sew something similar herself. The construction of clothing taught her to see creative projects in terms of design and pattern and how separate parts fit together to make a new whole. Today, pattern and design still play a big role in her creative vision overall, whether she is sewing a dress or doing mixed-media art.

For Ellene, creative thoughts are never far away. As she lies in bed before she goes to sleep, visions of projects float through her mind. She often works on something mentally for several days until she gets the chance to sit down and actually create it. Ellene sees this mental planning, dreaming and imagining stage as crucial to successful design. Ellene's creative space is in a corner of her living room. She likes that she can create while her family is around so she doesn't feel like she is stealing their time. Her space has evolved since she started her online business, and sometimes during a busy season her work spreads and takes over the living space. Her craft table sits beside a window with a peaceful view of the top of a huge one-hundred-year-old tree at the base of a hill outside her home. In the winter, she enjoys the spindly bare branches, while in the summer the lush, green leaves inspire her.

Getting to work is sometimes easy for Ellene, but sometimes it requires the use of personal rituals. Often she feels very excited about an idea she got earlier in the day while out walking or doing some housework. On those days, her pent-up creative energy drives her to her table where she immediately gathers her supplies and tools and begins to

create. But sometimes before she can get to work, Ellene cleans and organizes her art space. Her brain feels chaotic if her space is unorganized from her last project with bits and pieces of paper here, spools of thread there. On these days, organizing her space helps clear her mind. If she is facing a big project that she is especially nervous about, she will sit down and pray first. These rituals put the other tasks of the day behind her so she can focus on her art.

Ellene has taken time to impart her love of problem solving and creating something beautiful to her daughter, Sasha. Ellene taught Sasha how to sew when she was about six years old, just like Ellene's mom taught her. Knowing how to sew has served Ellene so well throughout her life that she wanted her daughter to share that knowledge. Together, Ellene and Sasha have made clothes, wire sculptures, game cartridge holders and tote bags. They have papier-mâchéd, painted on walls and redecorated rooms.

ELLENE'S ADVICE FOR MOTHERS WHO WANT TO DO ART:

"Make an art appointment with yourself after your children's bedtime or during nap time, because it's important that we make that time for ourselves to create."

Workshop

You have your basic tools and have carved out your space and time. Now it is time to do some mixed-media work. The projects in this chapter are designed to be completed over a twelve-week period. I have created Art Action Plans to help you keep on track to complete the twelve projects. The schedules are broken down so you could take between an hour and two hours to make art each day, six days a week. Each week you will be guided through the current week's project. Also, the suggested poetry and photography challenges will help prepare you for future projects, so you will keep a few balls in the air at once. You can do it— you have a Momma mind that's used to doing ten things at once!

If you have multiple young children, family issues, are pregnant or have a job outside the home, you may find the suggested time frame is too much for you. No problem—simply spread each week's work out over a two-week or even a month-long period. The goal is to get the projects done over time within the constraints of your actual life. Be realistic. The important thing is not speed, but your commitment to doing the work. And when you are done with all twelve projects, you will be glad that you did them regardless of how long it takes.

During the workshop, you may waver at times and feel like giving up. If so, reread your goals or action plan or even the previous chapters in this book for reinspiration. Take a week off after Week 6 if you need to. Regroup, review what you have made, tidy up your art space, do some household chores that need doing. But after a week, get back into your art.

The workshop projects are simple, but try to avoid the temptation to do a whole project in one sitting. Have patience. Be mindful of your long-term goals and your commitment to art. Avoid the temptation to rush ahead, as you risk burning out before you make it to the end of the twelve weeks. Remember Tortoise!

"There are many reasons why we are moved to make art. To communicate a message or to reveal some part of ourselves, to amuse others, to commemorate events and milestones, to come to a deeper understanding of inner feelings. And then there is the simple act of just making beauty. Art for art's sake, to give pleasure to the eye, to provide the spirit with a gentle place to rest and contemplate loveliness."

PAULA DION

Preparation Week

Before you start the workshop, take a week or two to arrange an environment conducive to creating:

1) Read the supply list for each project. Gather together what you have and buy or borrow anything you don't. Make sure you have everything in the Essential Toolbox (see below) handy and accessible. You'll need these materials for every project. Once you have these supplies on hand, you only have to worry about getting items specific to each week when the time comes.

2) Start collecting things to go in your art stash (see page 55).

3) Start writing your art vision statement and goals lists (see pages 20–21).

4) Take time to carve out and organize your art space (see page 30).

5) Rearrange your daily schedule to include art time. Identify your time stealers (see page 28). Cut them back or out of your week. Think about ways to find and prioritize your time. Line up baby-sitters. Tell your family your intentions so they are on board and supportive.

6) Make a music playlist for your iPod or gather CDs to inspire you as you work. Buy a new candle. Identify your rituals and make sure you have whatever you need for your creative atmosphere (see page 23).

7) Tell a friend or your spouse of your intention to complete this workshop. Or better still, enlist a friend to do the workshop at the same time. You can hold each other accountable (see page 22).

8) Buy or borrow from a friend or the library some poetry books to read. See page 126 for some suggestions.

Essential Toolbox

Color Tools: gesso, acrylic paint, water-soluble oil pastels, various size paintbrushes, mixing palette, water jar, cloth, 4B pencil, solvent ink (black, purple, green and red will do for all the projects), rubber stamps

Adhesives: glue stick, liquid glue, spray fixative

Altering Tools: scissors, steel ruler, craft knife, cutting mat, paper cutter, sandpaper, heat gun, awl

Art Stash: see page 55 (make sure to include some matte photo paper for ink-jet printers)

Equipment: camera, computer, ink-jet printer with scanning bed, photo processing software

BACKGROUNDS AND LISTS

No matter how large your art stash is, you can always add more of your own backgrounds to it. Your personalized backgrounds lend authenticity to your mixed-media work and ensure that you are not tempted to buy too many ready-made papers. While you'll use some of these backgrounds in subsequent projects, you will need some of them this week to create your to-do and baby-sitter lists.

CHALLENGES

Poetry

Read one poem each day. Read at least one poem aloud.

Photo

**Kids in Action (for Week 4—
        Vision Statement Banner)**

Make a list of what your kids do in everyday life—have lunch, color, read, play in their room, climb into the car, listen to an iPod, do homework, mow the lawn, talk on the phone…. Explain to your kids that you need a photo for an art project. Tell them that you will be moving about taking shots from many different angles and distances. Tell them to keep on doing what they are doing and not to pose and look at the camera. Explain that you want to make a record of their life. This explanation is especially important for older kids—you don't want to violate their budding personal boundaries.

SUGGESTED ART ACTION PLAN

Day 1
- PROJECT Read through this week's projects. Complete Backgrounds, step 1.
- POETRY Read a poem.
- PHOTOGRAPHY Make a list of your kids' activities.

Day 2
- PROJECT Backgrounds, step 2.
- POETRY Read a poem.
- PHOTOGRAPHY Take (at least) ten Kids in Action photos.
- RESEARCH Browse mixed-media Web sites or art blogs.

Day 3
- PROJECT Art Action Plan and Baby-sitter Lists, step 1 or 2.
- POETRY Read a poem.
- PHOTOGRAPHY Take (at least) ten Kids in Action photos.

Day 4
- PROJECT Backgrounds, steps 3–4 and Art Action Plan and Baby-sitter Lists, steps 3–4.
- POETRY Read a poem.
- PHOTOGRAPHY Take (at least) ten Kids in Action photos. Pick out and scan a photo of your younger self to use in Week 2.

Day 5
- POETRY Read a poem.
- RESEARCH Browse photography Web sites or art blogs.

Day 6
- PREPARATION Organize your craft space.
- PHOTOGRAPHY Take and upload photos.

Day 7
- Catch-up day.

BACKGROUNDS

Materials List

ESSENTIAL TOOLBOX PLUS ...
4 sheets regular computer paper
4 sheets colored cardstock
4 sheets junk mail paper

Preparation

★ Gather sheets of plain paper and
   junk mail.

★ Organize your craft space and get
   out supplies you need for this project.

1 Gather papers together and
spread them out on newspaper.
Paint the papers with gesso.
Let them dry.

2 Paint one side of all 12 gessoed
pages with various colors. Try each
of the painting techniques on pages
60–61. Let these dry.

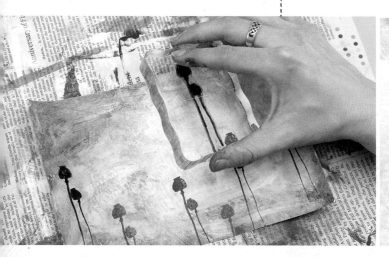

3 Gather up a variety of stamps. Choose some large
and graphic stamps and others that have more detail.
Use a few colors of ink, too. Working in a conveyor
belt fashion, randomly stamp some of the sheets,
leaving others blank.

4 Add water-soluble oil pastels to the edges of some
of the sheets. Blend with your finger.

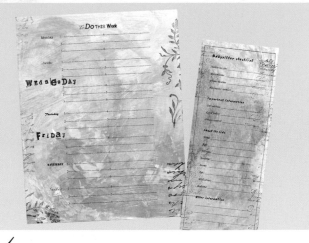

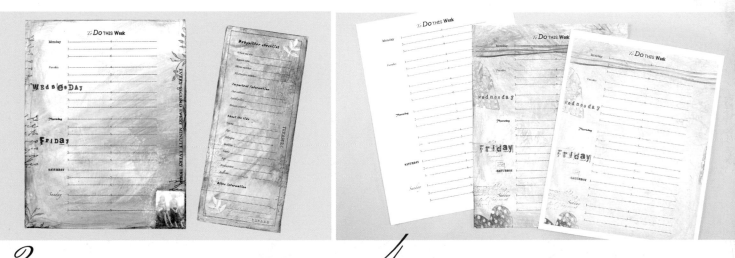

1 Create a layout on your computer for your Art Action Plan and (optional) Baby-sitter List. Pick a light-colored painted background paper. Print the blank document onto your background paper.

2 (Optional) Instead of printing, draw your list/ Art Action Plan directly onto the background paper with a charcoal pencil. Use stamps and printed words to decorate.

3 Stamp some words on the to do list. Add stamps to the borders of the page. Add water-soluble oil pastels to the edges of the paper and blend with your finger. Decorate with photos or punched images.

4 Now, scan this sheet back into your computer and save it as either a Word document or a JPEG file. Every week you can print out a blank copy of your Art Action Plan and add your to-do list to it.

POETRY JOURNAL

While you can scribble your poetic words in any old notebook or on scraps of paper, wouldn't it be more artistic to record them in a journal that you have decorated for that purpose? When you pull your personal poetry journal out of your bag and see your artwork and handle a notebook with a texture that you created, your own creation can spur you into action.

CHALLENGES

Poetry

Read a poem every other day.

Write a list of observations about your immediate surroundings. Brainstorm for three minutes, writing anything that comes to mind (without judgment) in your as yet undecorated poetry journal. Look for rhymes, slant rhymes, assonance and alliteration in your list. Focus on a different sense each day.

Photo

Front Shots (for Week 5—Butterfly Reminder)

Have the children smile, frown, look surprised, laugh, be serious—tell them you want to record a range of emotions. (Yes, talk like that even to very young children. It is amazing what they understand!)

SUGGESTED ART ACTION PLAN

Day 1
- PROJECT Read though the steps in this week's project. Get supplies ready. Complete Poetry Journal preparation.
- POETRY Read a poem. Write a list of sounds for three minutes.
- PHOTOGRAPHY Talk to your kids about taking Front Shot photos. Plan their outfits and locations.

Day 2
- PROJECT Poetry Journal, steps 1–2.
- POETRY Write a list of things you see for three minutes.
- PHOTOGRAPHY Take at least ten Front Shot photos.
- RESEARCH Browse photography Web sites or photography blogs.

Day 3
- PROJECT Poetry Journal, step 3.
- POETRY Read a poem. Write a list of tastes for three minutes.
- PHOTOGRAPHY Process last week's Kids in Action photos.

Day 4
- PROJECT Poetry Journal, step 4.
- POETRY Read a poem. Write a list of smells for three minutes.
- PHOTOGRAPHY Take at least ten Front Shot photos.

Day 5
- PROJECT Poetry Journal, steps 5–9.
- POETRY Read a poem. Write a list of touch-related words for three minutes.
- RESEARCH Browse mixed-media or art Web sites.

Day 6
- PREPARATION Organize your craft space.
- PROJECT Poetry Journal, step 10.
- PHOTOGRAPHY Take and upload this week's photos.

Day 7
- Catch-up day.

POETRY JOURNAL

Materials List

ESSENTIAL TOOLBOX PLUS ...
Old photo of self as child
Spiral-bound blank journal
Painted backgrounds (from Week 1)
Fabric
Copyright-free images, photos,
movie tickets, scrapbook papers
Button or other embellishment
Fibers

Preparation

✱ Buy fabric and scrapbook papers that
coordinate with the paints you have
chosen as your working palette.

✱ Buy a blank journal, preferably one with
a spiral binding (bookstores all have
journaling sections).

✱ Choose an old photo of yourself
(and any other photos of interest).

✱ Type some poetic words—a favorite
verse, quote, Bible verse or your
own words.

✱ Organize your craft space and get out
supplies you need for this project.

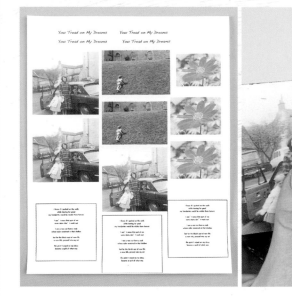

1 Scan your photo to your
computer. Resize it to fit on the
lower third of the journal cover. Type
up any words you're going to use.
Arrange everything on a page and
print it out on good matte photo
paper (I printed out multiple copies
of the images in case I made mistakes
and for use in later projects).

2 Trim images and words.
In order to make the focal photo
pop, ink its edges. The ink will
bleed into the paper on its own.

3 Go through your stash. Move your selections
around on the journal cover until you like the
composition. Leave it to sit out overnight. (If you
sleep on an idea before you commit to it, the right
or better answer can become visible.)

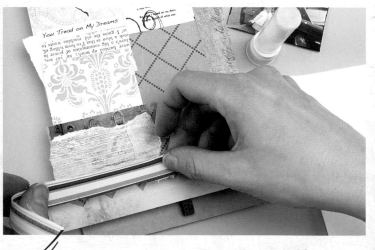

4 When you return to your journal, look for
anything that is not working. Rearrange a little,
adding in any new pieces that could make the layout
better. When you have settled on a final composition,
memorize where everything goes (take a photo of it if
you need to), then take everything off. Glue everything
down. Feel free to let things wander over the edge.

5 Trim the edges of the journal flush with a craft knife.

6 Stamp 3 to 4 images on the journal, not paying too much attention to the papers already in place.

7 To blend the book together, color the edges with water-soluble oil pastels and use your finger or a damp paintbrush to smudge.

8 Add some sparkle to the journal with a glue-on sequin (optional). Take the metal spiral out of the journal and paint the area around the holes.

9 Use découpage medium, matte finish sealer or spray fixative to seal everything.

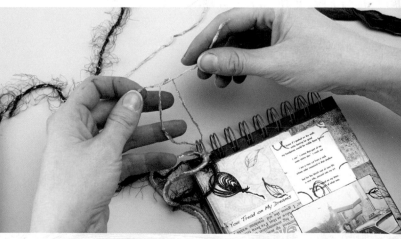

10 Reassemble the journal and tie fibers onto the spiral binding.

POETRY TOTE

This week you will make a bag to match your journal. If you house your journal in this little tote and bring it with you wherever you go, I guarantee you will be more likely to remember to jot down your ideas and to think poetically. As busy moms, we need all the tricks we can learn to get us working at our art. Don't panic if you have little skill in sewing, because this is a very simple project. Borrow a sewing machine if you must.

CHALLENGES

Poetry

Pick your favorite poet from the last two weeks of reading. Search the Web for more of the poet's poems to read. Write out a few lines that move you.

Think of minor events in your life—a visit by relatives, taking a bath with bath salts, going to the garden center to buy shrubs, writing Christmas cards, the first day of your child's kindergarten, installing a car seat while pregnant. Record the details: the temperature of the day, anything that was said, what your children were wearing, the color of the walls, how you felt. Attempt to write ten lines about the event. Reread Week 2's observations. See if any poetic lines come to mind from this list. When revising during the coming weeks, refer to the revision ideas on page 50.

Photo

Portraits (for Week 6—Nameplates)

Plan a photo shoot. Invite your kids to participate. Make it special! Invite each child to wear his or her favorite outfit or offer them a special treat when the photo shoot is over. Have them make lots of poses and facial expressions for fun. Enjoy focusing on each person. Try to get their eyes in focus. Take many pictures.

SUGGESTED ART ACTION PLAN

Day 1
- PROJECT Read though the steps in this week's project. Get supplies ready. Complete Poetry Tote, prep and step 1.
- POETRY Read a poem. Write a Minor Events word list.
- PHOTOGRAPHY Talk to your kids about the photo shoot. Plan outfits, time and locations.

Day 2
- PROJECT Poetry Tote, steps 2–6.
- POETRY Read a poem. Reread last week's observation words.
- PHOTOGRAPHY Process last week's Front Shots.

Day 3
- PROJECT Poetry Tote, steps 7–11.
- POETRY Read a poem.
- PHOTOGRAPHY Continue to process last week's Front Shots.
- RESEARCH Browse art-related Web sites or blogs.

Day 4
- PROJECT Poetry Tote, steps 12–15.
- POETRY Read a poem. Reread last week's observation words and this week's Minor Events words. Write a few lines.
- PHOTOGRAPHY Charge your camera's battery.

Day 5
- POETRY Write more lines about Minor Events—consult your word lists.
- RESEARCH Browse photography Web sites or art blogs.

Day 6
- PREPARATION Organize your craft space.
- PROJECT Read the list of supplies needed for next week.
- PHOTOGRAPHY Photo shoot day! Upload photos.

Day 7
- Catch-up day.

POETRY TOTE

Materials List

Fabric—at least 6 different patterns;
mix large and small patterns; cut into:

9 | 4" × 4" (10cm × 10cm) squares (front)

2 | 9" × 9" (23cm × 23cm) squares (back)

2 | 9" × 9" (23cm × 23cm) squares (lining)

2 | 4" × 19" (10cm × 48cm) rectangles
(handles)

3" × 3" (8cm × 8cm) cardboard square

Old photo of yourself (same as for
poetry journal)

Printable canvas sheet

Sewing machine

Thread

Iron

Fusible interfacing cut into:

2 | 9" × 9" (23cm × 23cm) squares

2 | 4" × 19" (10cm × 48cm) rectangles

Preparation

★ Choose your fabric.

★ Cut all of the fabric and interfacing.

★ Draw your 3" × 3" (8cm × 8cm) square
on a piece of cardboard and cut it out to
use as a template.

★ Print a copy of the old photo of yourself
from last week onto printable canvas.

★ Organize your craft space and get out
supplies you need for this project.

1 Trace the 3" × 3" (8cm × 8cm)
cardboard square on the back of
each small fabric square in its center.

2 Arrange the 9 small fabric squares
as they will appear on the bag. Make
sure to put your photo in the middle
of the middle row.

3 Sew the squares into 3 rows of 3 using the traced lines as a guide for
where to stitch. Press open the seams.

4 Sew the rows one to another to create a larger 9" × 9" (23cm × 23cm) square. Press open the seams.

5 Iron the fusible interfacing on the back of the patched square and on the fabric for the back of the bag. Trim the fusible interfacing even with the edges of the fabrics.

6 With right sides together, sew together the back and front of the bag along 3 edges—the bottom and 2 sides. Trim the edges to within ¼" (6mm) of the sewn edges and miter the corners. Turn the bag right side out. Set aside.

7 Sew the 2 pieces of lining fabric together along three sides, leaving a 2½" (6cm) gap in the middle of the bottom edge. Set aside.

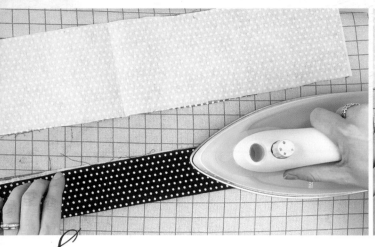

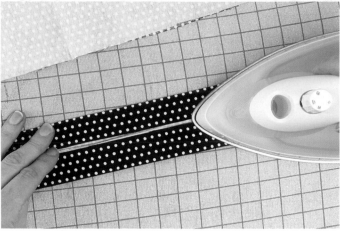

8 To make the handle, iron fusible interfacing on the back of the handle fabric. Fold the strip in half lengthwise and press.

9 Open the fabric back up. Fold the top edge down to meet the center crease. Repeat for the bottom edge. Press.

10 Fold the handle in half lengthwise again, sandwiching the edges inside, and press. Sew the seam shut. Repeat steps 8–10 for the other handle.

11 Pin the 2 ends of one handle to the top, unseamed edge of the bag, one on each side of the center square. Turn the bag over and pin the second handle in the same place on the back of the bag.

12 Place the bag, including the handles, inside the lining. Pin together the two raw top edges (the edge of the lining and the edge of the outer fabrics).

13 Now comes the tricky part. Sew around the mouth of the bag about ¼" (6mm) from the edge to attach the lining, making sure to double-sew over the handles to give them added strength.

14 Turn the bag inside out by pulling it through the small opening in the bottom of the lining.

15 Hand sew the opening shut. Tuck the lining into the bag and press to make it look a little neater. Put your journal in the bag and remember to bring it with you wherever you go!

VISION STATEMENT BANNER

This project gets you to think about your vision and goals. It is one thing to contemplate setting goals, but it is another to publicly display them! This week you will make a wall hanging that reflects your vision so you can easily reread it and recharge. Your wall hanging will also include a detachable goals list, giving you the freedom to change and grow, so you are not locked into looking at a list that you have outgrown.

CHALLENGES

Poetry

Listen to poetry for five minutes each day this week.

Read at least one poem out loud to a friend or family member.

Open a novel to any page and write in your journal a list of twenty random words from the chapter you landed in. Use these words to spark a poem.

Reread and revise this week's poem and any words from Week 3.

Photo

Events (for Week 7—Altered Storybook)

Plan to take a series of photos that record an individual event (e.g., doing an art activity, visiting Granny, attending a show or recital, going to chess club, sailing). Think of an event that has a beginning, middle and end. Take shots as the event unfolds—don't worry about getting the perfect shot. Snapshots are good. Shoot more photos than you think you may need.

SUGGESTED ART ACTION PLAN

Day 1
- PROJECT Read though the steps in this week's project. Get supplies ready. Complete preparation.
- POETRY Listen to poetry for five minutes.
- PHOTOGRAPHY Plan events to photograph. Process photos from last week's photo shoot.

Day 2
- PROJECT Vision Statement Banner, steps 1–2.
- POETRY Listen to poetry for five minutes. Revise Minor Events poems from last week.
- PHOTOGRAPHY Take at least ten Events photos.

Day 3
- PROJECT Vision Statement Banner, step 3.
- POETRY Listen to poetry for five minutes. Create a word list from a novel.
- PHOTOGRAPHY Take at least ten Events photos.
- RESEARCH Browse photography Web sites or blogs.

Day 4
- PROJECT Vision Statement Banner, step 4.
- POETRY Listen to poetry for five minutes. Write a poem based on your novel list.
- PHOTOGRAPHY Send photos from last week's photo shoot for printing.

Day 5
- POETRY Listen to poetry for five minutes. Revise last week's Minor Events lines.
- RESEARCH Browse mixed-media Web sites or art blogs.
- PHOTOGRAPHY Take at least ten Events photos.

Day 6
- PROJECT Vision Statement Banner, steps 5–9. Read the list of supplies for next week.
- POETRY Listen to poetry for five minutes. Read aloud to someone. Revise this week's novel list poem.
- PREPARATION Organize your craft space.
- PHOTOGRAPHY Take and upload this week's photos.

Day 7
- Catch-up day.

BANNER

Materials List

ESSENTIAL TOOLBOX PLUS ...
Kids in Action photos (see page 69)
Wire-edged ribbon
Fabric scraps left over from
last week's project
18" × 8" (46cm × 20cm) piece of fabric
18" × 8" (46cm × 20cm) piece of
fusible interfacing left over from last
week's project
Iron
Background papers (from Week 1)
Ephemera
Stamped trimmed butterfly image
Ribbon
Rub-ons
Sewing machine
Fibers
2 wooden dowels
Velcro

Preparation

* Type your vision statement and goals
  list (see pages 20–21).

* Print them over a Kids in Action
  photo onto matte photo paper.

* Rummage through your fabric and
  paper stash, choose color scheme.

* Pick a fabric for the background.

* Cut the fabric and a piece of fusible
  interfacing to size.

* Organize your craft space and get out
  supplies you need for this project.

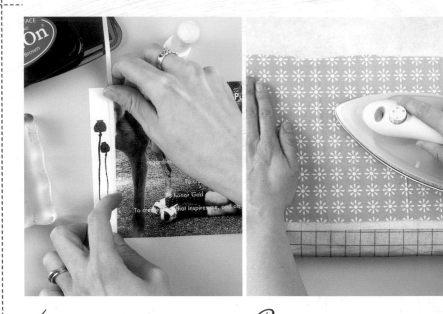

1 Trim three sides of the vision statement and goals list photos and stamp on the white edge of the final side. Glue on some ribbon or fabric to decorate the edge.

2 Iron a piece of fusible interfacing to the back of your fabric. Trim to fit.

3 Arrange your materials and photo on the banner. Move images around. Leave the composition alone overnight.

4 When you see your banner the next day, rearrange it if necessary. When satisfied with the composition, glue everything in place. Make sure to leave a blank spot where you can attach your goals.

5 Make a dowel pocket by folding back the top edge of the fabric. Fold about 1¼" (3cm) to the back. Sew it in place, leaving both ends open to insert your dowel. Repeat for the bottom edge.

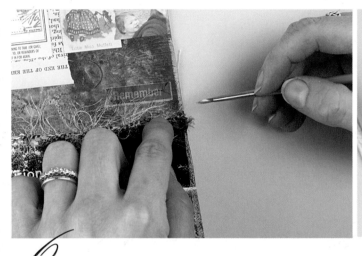

6 Using a small paintbrush to spread the glue, attach a fiber along each sewn seam and across the top edge of the photograph.

7 Put a small amount of watery paint on a rag and rub it over the dowel, staining the wood.

8 Slide the dowels into their pockets. Tie your wire-edged ribbon to both ends of the top dowel in order to hang up your artwork.

9 Attach one side of a piece of Velcro to the goals list photo and the other to the space left on the Vision Statement Banner. As your goals change you can also change out the goals list.

BUTTERFLY REMINDER

We all need a little sparkle of inspiration in our home. For this project, think carefully about what you need to be reminded of daily—that particular something that doesn't yet come naturally. For me it is writing. While I remember to take my camera with me and photograph my kids, I often forget to write down the little words and ideas that cross my mind. I need a reminder. For you, it might be a reminder to get your paints out, or to check art blogs or to take your camera with you.

CHALLENGES

Poetry

Record yourself reading the poem you wrote last week. Listen to the recording.

Read half of a book of poetry over the course of the week.

Look at the Events photos you took last week (Week 4). Write a short, ten-line children's story (for Week 7), beginning with, "Once there was a little girl/boy/two sisters…." Write it in language appropriate to your children's ages.

Revise this week's poem.

Photo

Day in the Life (for Week 9—Poetry Scrapbook)

Do a Day in the Life shoot. In Week 9 you will be making a scrapbook of some routine events. Here are some theme ideas: first day at school or driving, day out at the zoo, favorite toy, bedtime routine, working on a craft together. Look around—observe the things you do on that day. Start taking photos in the morning and continue all day. Shoot breakfast, the computer, favorite mugs, the car, laundry, the event itself. Take photos even of subjects that don't seem very inspiring. You never know—once you start processing, you may see something interesting emerge.

SUGGESTED ART ACTION PLAN

Day 1
- PROJECT Butterfly Reminder, prep and step 1.
- POETRY Read a poetry book.
- PHOTOGRAPHY Process Events photos from last week.

Day 2
- PROJECT Butterfly Reminder, steps 2–4.
- POETRY Reread last week's novel-list poem and record yourself reading it.
- PHOTOGRAPHY Process Events photos. Take at least ten Day in the Life photos.

Day 3
- PROJECT Butterfly Reminder, steps 5–12.
- POETRY Read a poetry book.
- PHOTOGRAPHY Take at least ten Day in the Life photos.
- RESEARCH Browse photography Web sites or blogs.

Day 4
- PROJECT Butterfly Reminder, steps 13–18.
- POETRY Listen to your recording of your own poem. Look at last week's Events photos and start to write your children's story.
- PHOTOGRAPHY Take at least ten Day in the Life photos.

Day 5
- POETRY Read a poetry book. Look at last week's Events photos and work on your children's story.
- RESEARCH Browse mixed-media Web sites or art blogs.

Day 6
- PROJECT Read ahead on the supplies for next week.
- POETRY Read a poetry book.
- PREPARATION Organize your craft space.
- PHOTOGRAPHY Take and upload this week's photos.

Day 7
- Catch-up day.

REMINDER

Materials List

ESSENTIAL TOOLBOX PLUS ...

Copyright-free butterfly image resized
to approximately 4" (10cm)

Printout of motivating words

Balsa wood—sold in strips in craft stores
(alternatively you could use regular
wood strips, but you would need a
woodcutting device)

Small star punch

Background paper

Front shot image of child (from Week 2)
resized to about 1" (3cm)

Eyelets

24-gauge jewelry wire

Wire cutter

Beads (optional)

Drill with $\frac{1}{8}$" (ISO 3.2mm) drill bit

Preparation

★ Create a document with 2 copies of a
  butterfly image (you can substitute a bird
  or other animal), the front shot photo of
  your child and inspiring words.

★ Organize your craft space and get out
  supplies you need for this project.

1 Print out the words and images you need. Cut everything out.

2 Cut out a small rectangle of balsa wood using your craft knife.
This piece will hang underneath your finished butterfly. Cut out a
section of one butterfly image to fit the small rectangle.

3 Glue the rectangle of paper onto the rectangle of balsa wood. Glue the intact butterfly onto an uncut piece of balsa wood.

4 Use a craft knife to trim the balsa wood around the butterfly. This takes a little time and patience, especially when cutting against the wood grain. With medium pressure, run the knife over and over along the outline of the butterfly. Don't expect the edges to be completely smooth—you will sand them later.

5 Paint a thin wash of gesso over the butterfly and rectangle. Let it dry or dry it quickly with a heat gun.

6 With solvent ink, stamp a background or word stamp on top of the gessoed images.

7 Punch out 3–4 paper stars from one of your background papers.

8 Glue the front shot of your child on one wing of the butterfly. Glue the stars on the other wing, and your words on the rectangular piece of balsa.

9 Sand lightly over the image's surface. Sand the edges of the butterfly so the paper melds with the wood.

10 Color the body of the butterfly with one color of water-soluble oil pastel and the edges with another. Blend with your fingers. With a soft pencil, doodle the edges of the butterfly, echoing the design.

11 Paint the back and sides of the piece. Let it dry. You may need to reapply your water-soluble oil pastels on the edges after painting.

12 Spray or paint both pieces with fixative.

13 Use a drill and a ¹/₈" (ISO 3.2mm) drill bit to make four small holes—one hole in each of the two top wings and one in each of the bottom wings. Then line up one long side of the small rectangle under the butterfly and drill two holes on its top edge corresponding to the two bottom wing holes. Finally, drill a hole in the bottom center of the small rectangle. Glue eyelets into the holes.

14 Cut a piece of wire long enough to reach from one top wing to the other with a little extra—this will be the handle. Thread one end through one of the top eyelets and wrap it around itself to secure. Thread on enough coordinating beads to cover the entire length of the handle wire (optional). Secure the other end to the other top eyelet.

15 Thread 3 beads onto a headpin for a dangle. Using needle-nose pliers, make an open loop with the open end of the headpin.

16 Trim off any excess wire. Close the loop.

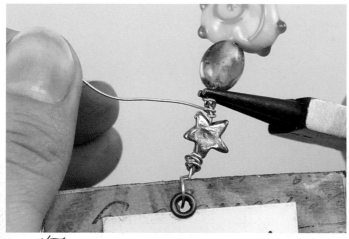

17 Cut a small length of wire. Attach one end of the wire to the bottom hole on the small rectangle. Thread a bead and then the dangle onto the wire. Secure the bead and dangle by looping the wire back on itself and then wrapping it. Trim any excess.

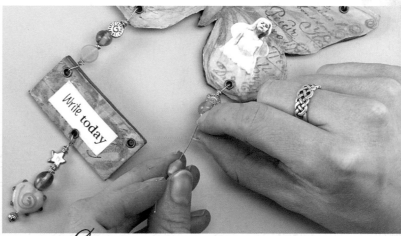

18 Cut 2 small, equal lengths of wire. Attach one to each of the bottom holes on the butterfly. Thread several beads onto each, making sure that both sides remain of equal length. Attach the 2 remaining ends of wire to the 2 remaining holes in the top of the small rectangle. Wrap to secure.

Lily Kate

NAMEPLATES

Children love to look at pictures of themselves, and they love to be included in your world. Why not satisfy both of these desires by making some art about them and for them? This week you will make something for each of your children. They will love their personalized nameplates.

CHALLENGES

Poetry

Read the rest of the book of poetry you started last week. Look for an underlying theme in the book.

Write outdoors, regardless of the weather.

Write about the sounds, the movement, the colors.

Read this week's poem aloud to yourself.

Revise as needed.

Revise your children's story (for Week 7).

Photo

Portraits 2 (for Week 8—Canvas Art)

Plan another photo shoot with your kids. Change the location or time of day. Take individual photos and photos of sibling groups.

SUGGESTED ART ACTION PLAN

Day 1
- PROJECTS Read though the steps in this week's project. Get supplies ready. Complete Nameplates preparation step.
- POETRY Read a poetry book. Write a word list outdoors.
- PHOTOGRAPHY Plan the photo shoot.

Day 2
- PROJECT Nameplates, step 1.
- POETRY Write some lines based on yesterday's word list outdoors.
- PHOTOGRAPHY Process Day in the Life photos from last week.

Day 3
- PROJECT Nameplates, steps 2–5.
- POETRY Read a poetry book.
- RESEARCH Browse photography Web sites or blogs.

Day 4
- PROJECT Nameplates, steps 6–9.
- POETRY Revise this week's lines.
- PHOTOGRAPHY Read a how-to book or Web site. Continue to process Day in the Life photos from last week.

Day 5
- POETRY Read a poetry book. Revise last week's story.
- RESEARCH Browse mixed-media Web sites or art blogs.
- PHOTOGRAPHY Charge your camera's batteries.

Day 6
- PROJECT Read ahead on the supplies needed for next week.
- POETRY Revise your children's story for next week's project.
- PREPARATION Organize your craft space.
- PHOTOGRAPHY Portrait photo shoot no. 2. Upload photos.

Day 7
- Catch-up day.

NAMEPLATES

Materials List

ESSENTIAL TOOLBOX PLUS ...

6" × 8" (15cm × 20cm) canvas board

Painted papers

Scrapbook papers

4" × 6" (10cm × 15cm) landscape portrait photo

Child's name, printed

Wooden letter

Floral stamp

Drill with $1/8$" (ISO 3.2mm) drill bit

Eyelet

Wire

Child's portrait (from Week 3)

Preparation

★ Pick the portrait photos up from the printer.

★ Print your child's name in a nice font (I used a color-filled text box).

★ Organize your craft space and get out supplies you need for this project.

1 Trim the printed name. Rummage through your stash looking for papers to complement the photo you are using. Try jarring colors or ones you would never think to use. Cut everything down so the pieces fit together on the canvas. Tear some strips for a slightly different look. Move the pieces around on the canvas until you like the composition. Leave it overnight.

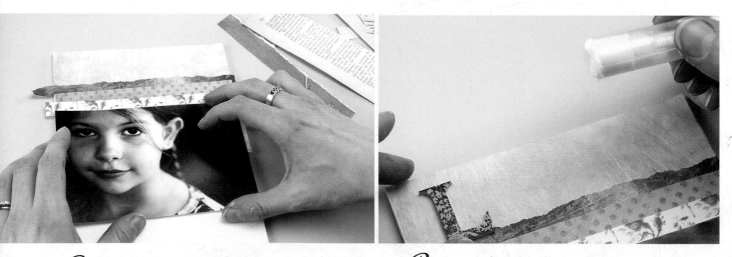

2 Rearrange the papers until you are totally happy with your composition. Glue all of the pieces down. To keep your hands glue-free, use a piece of paper to press items down. Trim everything flush with the edges of the canvas.

3 Use an intricate stamp on your wooden letter and stamp with solvent ink. Glue the letter onto your canvas board.

4 Sand the edges of the board so the paper blends with it. Color the edges with water-soluble oil pastels, then smudge with your finger.

5 Paint the edges of the piece.

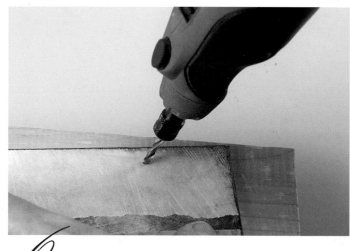

6 Drill holes on the top for the handle. The holes should be 1½" (38mm) in from the edge and ¼" (6mm) down from the top. You can use a household drill.

7 Use liquid glue to secure eyelets in the holes.

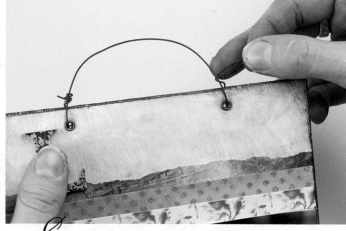

8 Push the end of the wire through the eyelet and wrap it around itself to secure. Repeat for the other side.

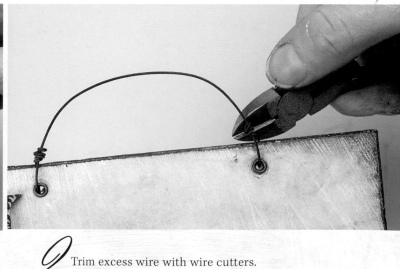

9 Trim excess wire with wire cutters.

Annie loves drawing!

ALTERED STORYBOOK

If you have been a mom for more than a year, you have probably read so many kid's stories that you could write your own. Well, here is your chance! You are going to write and decorate a book for your child, perhaps even a book about your child. When I make these books, my kids ask me to read them over and over, delighting in being the central character in a fanciful story. What child wouldn't?

CHALLENGES

Poetry

Listen to a poem each day this week. Which poem speaks to you? Why?

Look at the Day in the Life photos you took in Week 5. Write about your daily life or events (for Week 9 project)—where you are, what colors you see, what time of day it is, what you are doing, who is there. Now, imagine your child comes in the door—what does he say or do? Describe him. You will be making a scrapbook in Week 9. Anything that is special and concerns the details of the life of your children is worthy of both poetry and a poetic scrapbook.

Revise last week's poem.

Photo

About Me Photos (for future projects)

Pretend you are going to tell someone about yourself through photos. Take photos of your favorite things—your books, decorations, art supplies, gifts given by someone special—and special places—school, church, the tree under which you sit, a restaurant, the cinema.

SUGGESTED ART ACTION PLAN

Day 1
- PROJECT Altered Storybook, preparation and steps 1 and 2.
- POETRY Listen to a poem. Revise last week's outdoor poem.

Day 2
- PROJECT Altered Storybook, step 3.
- POETRY Listen to a poem. Look at your Day in the Life photos from Week 5 and write a word list.
- PHOTOGRAPHY Process your photo shoot no. 2 photos from last week.

Day 3
- POETRY Listen to a poem.
- RESEARCH Browse mixed-media Web sites or blogs.
- PHOTOGRAPHY Take ten About Me photos.

Day 4
- PROJECT Altered Storybook, step 4.
- POETRY Listen to a poem. Look at your Day in the Life photos and write some lines (for Week 9).
- PHOTOGRAPHY Process your photos from photo shoot no. 2. Send Day in the Life photos (for Week 9) to be printed.

Day 5
- POETRY Work on your Day in the Life poem (for Week 9).
- RESEARCH Browse photography Web sites or art blogs.
- PHOTOGRAPHY Take ten About Me photos.

Day 6
- PROJECT Altered Storybook, steps 5–8. Read ahead for the supplies needed for next week.
- POETRY Listen to a poem.
- PREPARATION Organize your craft space.
- PHOTOGRAPHY Take and upload ten About Me photos.

Day 7
- Catch-up day.

STORYBOOK

Materials List

ESSENTIAL TOOLBOX PLUS ...
Photo of your kids' events (from Week 4)
Children's story (from Week 5)
Old board book with 5–6 page spreads
Embellishments

Preparation

★ Choose an old board book.

★ Organize your craft space and get out
  supplies you need for this project.

1 You should have already written your children's story
and taken the daily life photos in previous weeks. Resize the photos to fit in the board book and print them
out. Trim the photos. Print a copy of your children's
story in an interesting font.

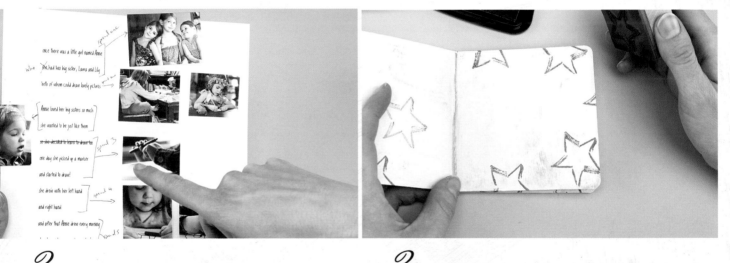

2 Lay the photos out and decide which line of the
story goes with which photo. Aim for approximately 2
lines per page spread. Edit the text as necessary (you
will have to reprint your text).

3 Prep the book. Sand the pages, leaving some
of the glossy surface intact. Decide on the color
scheme for your book. Paint the pages of the book
with gesso mixed with a little bit of acrylic paint,
taking off some of the paint with a cloth. When dry,
stamp background images on the pages. Use a
different stamp for each page. If needed, gesso
over these images to tone them down.

4 Trim the lines of the story and glue them and the photos in place.

5 Lightly sand your photos so the color from the photos blends into the dried paint and gesso.

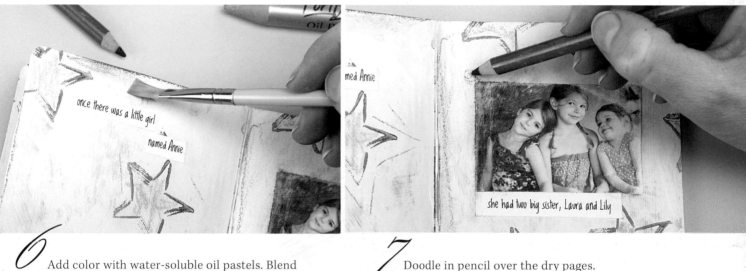

6 Add color with water-soluble oil pastels. Blend everything with water or just use your finger.

7 Doodle in pencil over the dry pages.

8 Glue embellishments to the outer cover and binding. Coordinate your embellishments with your content. My book is about my little girl's drawing, so I glued a pencil embellishment to the binding.

CANVAS ART

If you have never worked on stretched canvas before, you are in for a treat. You will love that you don't have to worry about framing a canvas. Once you have completed the art, you are ready to hang it up! This canvas art project is kind of like a scrapbook page, but for the wall. Get ready to display your child bathed in color and images as you tell a visual story of a moment in her life.

CHALLENGES

Poetry

Research poems about children or childhood online. Read at least five.

Write about your experiences as a mother. Think of individual moments, not motherhood as a whole—the moment you learned you were pregnant, the birth, the first time she said "Momma." Write down details of the times, places, series of events. Juxtapose those memories with where you are at now in your mothering. How have you grown?

Revise your poem from Week 7.

Photo

No People (for future projects)

Take pictures with no people. Look for patterns, textures and beautiful colors in the world around you.

SUGGESTED ART ACTION PLAN

Day 1
- PROJECT Read though the steps in this week's project. Get supplies ready. Complete Canvas Art preparation step.
- POETRY Find poems related to childhood. Write word lists about motherhood.
- PHOTOGRAPHY Take ten No People photos.

Day 2
- PROJECT Canvas Art, steps 1–3.
- POETRY Write some lines about motherhood.
- PHOTOGRAPHY Process your About Me photos from last week.

Day 3
- PROJECT Canvas Art, steps 4–6.
- POETRY Read poetry.
- RESEARCH Browse mixed-media Web sites or blogs.

Day 4
- PROJECT Canvas Art, step 7.
- POETRY Revise last week's Day in the Life poems.
- PHOTOGRAPHY Take ten No People photos.

Day 5
- POETRY Read poetry. Revise your motherhood poem.
- RESEARCH Browse mixed-media Web sites or art blogs.
- PHOTOGRAPHY Continue to process your About Me photos.

Day 6
- PROJECT Canvas Art, step 8. Read ahead for the supplies needed for next week.
- POETRY Revise your Day in the Life poem for Week 9.
- PREPARATION Organize your craft space.
- PHOTOGRAPHY Take ten No People photos and upload them.

Day 7
- Catch-up day.

CANVAS ART

Materials List

ESSENTIAL TOOLBOX PLUS ...

8" × 10" (20cm × 25cm) prestretched
canvas

Swirly, decorative rubber stamp

Square-shaped portrait of your child from
photo shoot no. 2

Buttons

Fibers

Hammer

Beads

Nails that fit through the bead holes

Large star punch

Rub-on word

Preparation

★ Choose a portrait of your child to
feature in this artwork.

★ Print a copy of the photo and trim it
to a square.

★ Decide on a color scheme for your piece.

★ Organize your craft space and get out
supplies you need for this project

1 With a large paintbrush, paint random blocks of five different colors that complement the focal image photo. Paint the sides of the canvas, too. Let the paint dry.

2 Paint a thin layer of gesso over the entire canvas. Before the gesso dries, wipe some of the gesso off the canvas with a rag or paper towel.

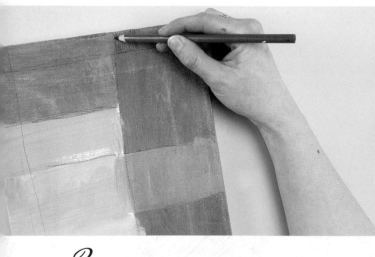

3 Once the gesso has dried, draw pencil lines where the colors meet plus some extra boxes.

4 Add an extra layer of gesso to the bottom third of the canvas. Let it dry. Stamp a background stamp across the bottom edge of the canvas.

5 Reinforce your pencil lines. Smudge the lines with your finger. Add water-soluble pastels to the edges of the canvas. You can also add pastels to the interior of the canvas.

6 Get out your papers. Move them around the canvas until you have a pleasing composition, using punched stars and other embellishments. Leave them overnight.

7 Rearrange the composition. When you decide on the final layout, glue everything in place. Add some rub-on words to enhance the meaning of the piece. Add some texture by wrapping some fibers multiple times around the canvas. Tie or glue the fibers in the back. If any of your papers go over the edge, trim them.

8 Hammer a beaded nail into the middle of the top edge of the canvas. Hammer in two more beaded nails on each side of the first one, spaced evenly across the top. Repeat with five more nails on the bottom of the canvas.

POETRY SCRAPBOOK

Hopefully by now you feel a little more comfortable with the idea of writing poetry about your life. Now is the time to combine your words with your images and mixed media in a scrapbook that reflects a small portion of your life. Your photos and words will offer the world a piece of you in a tangible, personal form. There is nothing as lovely as holding your own handmade book!

CHALLENGES

Poetry

Research new places on the Internet to listen to poetry. Download a recording of a poetry reading. Listen for ten minutes every day. Write a poem about one of your children (for Week 11). Describe his features, hair color, favorite toy or activity. Think of yourself as a child—can you see any similarities? Are there any events in your childhood that you would like to tell this child about? Can you imagine being friends with your child? What kind of playmate would you have been? Let these musings direct your words.

Revise last week's motherhood experience poems.

Photo

Poetic Photos (for Week 12—Poetry Box)

Look ahead at Week 12's project for an idea of photos you need to take. Pick a subject (e.g., your house, a pond, a tree, your kid's bike) and study it. Photograph it from every angle—get on your knees; stand up on a chair and shoot down; lie down on the ground and shoot up.

SUGGESTED ART ACTION PLAN

Day 1
- PROJECT Read through the steps in this week's project. Get supplies ready. Complete Poetry Scrapbook preparation step.
- POETRY Listen to poetry for ten minutes. Write a word list about a child.
- PHOTOGRAPHY Decide on a subject to study.

Day 2
- PROJECT Poetry Scrapbook, step 1.
- POETRY Listen to poetry for ten minutes.
- PHOTOGRAPHY Take at least ten Poetic photos.
- RESEARCH Browse photography Web sites or blogs.

Day 3
- PROJECT Poetry Scrapbook, steps 2–6.
- POETRY Listen to poetry for ten minutes. Write lines about a child.
- PHOTOGRAPHY Take at least ten Poetic photos.

Day 4
- PROJECT Continue work on Poetry Scrapbook, steps 2–6.
- POETRY Listen to poetry for ten minutes. Revise last week's motherhood poem.
- PHOTOGRAPHY Take at least ten Poetic photos.

Day 5
- PROJECT Continue work on Poetry Scrapbook, steps 2–6.
- POETRY Listen to poetry for ten minutes.
- RESEARCH Browse mixed-media Web sites or art blogs.
- PHOTOGRAPHY Process last week's No People photos.

Day 6
- PROJECT Poetry Scrapbook, steps 7–8.
- POETRY Listen to poetry for ten minutes. Revise your child poem.
- PHOTOGRAPHY Take and upload Poetic photos.

Day 7
- Catch-up day.

SCRAPBOOK

Materials List

ESSENTIAL TOOLBOX PLUS …

Approximately 12 8" × 8" (20cm × 20cm)
background pages and at least 1 half sheet

3–4 Day in the Life photos (from Week 5)

Day in the Life poem (from Week 7)

Spray adhesive

Photo to distress (see page 44)

Sewing machine

Fibers

Colored gel pen

Shaped punches

Embellishments

Hole punch (optional)

Dowel

Needle and craft floss

Brads

Preparation

★ Pick up your Day in the Life photos
   from the printer.

★ Alter the photos using the techniques on
   page 44.

★ Print your Day in the Life poem onto a
   full sheet of painted background paper.

★ Organize your craft space and get out

1 Rummage through your art stash and pick out the papers to use as the pages of your scrapbook, including your Day in the Life poem printed on a painted sheet. Trim all to 8" × 8" (20cm × 20cm). Over the next few days you will work on a few pages at a time deciding which photos, words and embellishments will go on which page. If you need more painted background papers, create some by using the techniques on pages 60–61 and 70).

2 Divide the backgrounds into groups of 4 and plan on working on each 4 over the next 3 days. Consider these ideas when embellishing your pages: You can adhere several backgrounds to each other to create a new background. On another spread, consider creating a fold-out journaling insert from a paper bag using rub-on letters.

3 On yet another spread, include small snippets from the Day in the Life poem by stamping with letter stamps or writing with a colored gel pen. You can also attach photos to the pages with brads.

4 Machine stitch one of the photos onto a half sheet background page.

5 Layer different types of fabric and papers onto each other to create new textures. Gesso over all of them. Use rubber stamps, rub-ons, pencil and oil pastels to embellish your pages.

6 Punch decorative holes in a page so you can see another page through the holes. Use playing or decorative cards layered onto cardstock to embellish your pages.

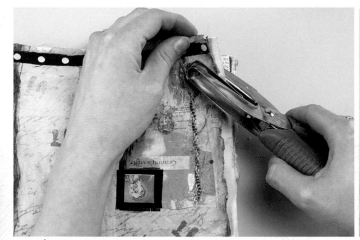

7 Take some time to order your book. Lay out the finished pages on the floor in a line and let the pages tell a story. Now is the time to adhere the pages to one another. In a well-ventilated area, lay the cover page on its front and spray with adhesive spray. Quickly lay page 2 on top. Repeat for pages 3 and 4, 5 and 6 and so on for all 12 sheets. When you have done that, line up the pages and use an awl or hole punch to punch three holes along one edge of the book (you may need to do just a few pages at a time). Stamp a dowel.

8 Thread a large needle with craft floss. Sew up from the back of the book to the front through the top hole, leaving a long tail of floss. Sew around the dowel and back down through the same hole. Bring the floss up from the back through the middle hole to the front, around the dowel and back down through the middle hole again. Finally, sew up through the bottom hole, around the dowel, and back down to the back of the book. Pull the floss tight and tie the two ends together in back of the book.

FAIRY FINDINGS BOX

Your children are again the subject matter of this interactive project. If you have girls like mine, they will spend hours arranging and rearranging the little details in their fairy findings box. If you have boys, an alternative to fairies for your box could be flying wizards or superheroes.

CHALLENGES

Poetry

Listen to a poem every day.

Look ahead at Week 12's project. Use the photos you took last week (Week 9) as a prompt for your poem (for Week 12). Brainstorm all the words that the photos say. Is there a theme? Can you find a metaphor for a life lesson?

Revise the poem about your child from last week (for Week 11).

Photo

Close-ups

Take close-ups this week. Shoot the details of life. Take pictures of your children's hands, feet, noses, smiles. Get close.

SUGGESTED ART ACTION PLAN

Day 1
- PROJECT Read though the steps in this week's project. Get supplies ready. Complete Fairy Findings Box preparation and steps 1–3.
- POETRY Listen to a poem.
- RESEARCH Browse photography Web sites or blogs.
- PHOTOGRAPHY Process last week's Poetic photos.

Day 2
- PROJECT Fairy Findings Box, steps 4–7.
- POETRY Listen to a poem. Revise last week's child poem.
- PHOTOGRAPHY Take at least ten Close-up photos.

Day 3
- POETRY Listen to a poem. Generate a word list from last week's poetic photos.
- PHOTOGRAPHY Take at least ten Close-up photos.

Day 4
- PROJECT Fairy Findings Box, steps 8–12.
- POETRY Listen to a poem. Write a poem from your word list.
- PHOTOGRAPHY Take at least ten Close-up photos.

Day 5
- POETRY Listen to a poem.
- PHOTOGRAPHY Continue to process last week's Poetic photos.
- RESEARCH Browse mixed-media Web sites or art blogs.

Day 6
- PROJECT Fairy Findings Box, steps 13–17.
- POETRY Listen to a poem. Revise child poem for Week 11.
- PHOTOGRAPHY Take and upload photos.

Day 7
- Catch-up day.

FAIRY BOX

Materials List

ESSENTIAL TOOLBOX PLUS ...

Wooden rectangle or house-shaped box
(I used a Melissa & Doug dollhouse box)

Cigar box

Photos of child's face

Cardboard

4 jump rings

Wire

Wire cutter

Beads

Drill with ⅛" (ISO 3.2mm) drill bit

Fairy findings (anything that sparkles
or that your child gifted to you)

Cloth flower

Buttons

Preparation

★ If you have not done so already, purchase
  wooden rectangle or house-shaped box.

★ Choose your color scheme, pick out a
  large sheet of background paper.

★ Organize your craft space and get out
  supplies you need for this project.

1 Sand the inside of your house box lightly. Paint the cigar box and the inside of the house with acrylic paint. Dry with a heat gun and apply a second coat.

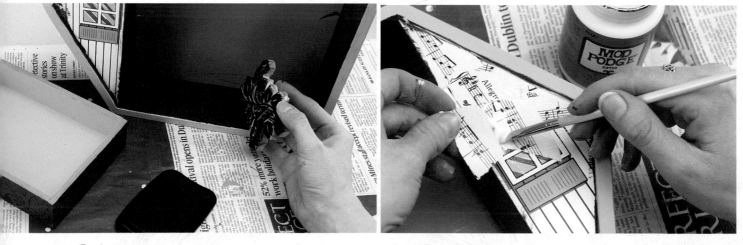

2 Stamp the inside walls (but not the back wall), ceiling and floor of the house and the outside of the cigar box with a decorative stamp.

3 Tear up a piece of background paper. Use liquid glue to stick the pieces to the front of the roof. Paint the glue both under and over the paper.

4 Cut a piece of background paper to fit the back wall of the house. Punch or cut flowers and stems (or any other embellishment you'd like to add) from other background papers.

5 Glue the paper embellishments to the background paper you cut in step 4. Outline the flowers with pencil and add water-soluble oil pastels.

6 Glue the finished background into the house.

7 Finish embellishing your boxes and decorate the exterior of the house with papers, fabric flowers, buttons and water-soluble oil pastels. Seal everything with fixative.

8 Choose a photo of your child's face (I made two fairies, one for each of my daughters). Resize them so the faces are approximately ¾" (19mm) and print. Trim close to the faces. Paint and stamp the hair.

9 Gather some background paper scraps. Freehand draw on background paper dress, foot, wing, arm and hand shapes for your fairy. Trim.

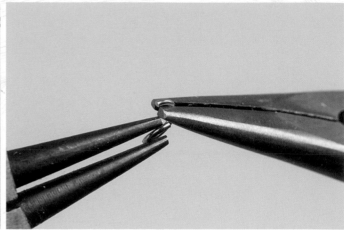

10 Glue the paper cut-outs and faces onto some cardboard in the shape of a fairy. Trim. Paint the back and sides with acrylic paint. When dry, use your awl to poke a hole in the hand and the wing.

11 Make a beaded dangle as you did in steps 15–16 of the Butterfly Reminder project (see Week 5, page 91). Twist 4 jump rings open with two sets of pliers by holding one side of the opening still while you pull the other side back.

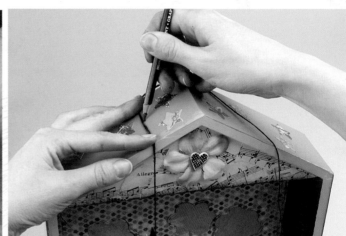

12 (Optional) Attach a jump ring to the hole in the hand. Add the beaded dangle. Twist the jump ring closed. With the other jump ring, attach a dangly embellishment (in this case a Shrinky Dink button) to the bottom of the beaded dangle. Twist the jump rings closed.

13 Hold up your fairy inside the box and decide where you would like it to hang. Make a pencil mark on the ceiling where you would like to attach it. Tie a small weight to the end of a piece of string to use as a plumb line. Use the plumb line to find the spot on the roof directly above the pencil mark on the ceiling. Do this by hanging the plumb line straight down in front of the house and moving it until it lines up with the ceiling mark. Mark the spot on the roof in back of the string. Then measure the distance from the front edge of your house in to the ceiling mark. Measure that same distance in from the mark on the edge of the roof and mark with a pencil. (Of course, if you have a drill bit long enough to drill all the way through both ceiling and roof or you are using a simple rectangular box, you can skip all this.)

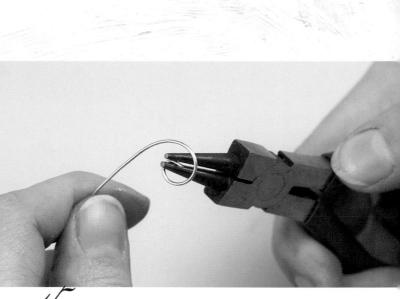

14 Drill a hole through both the dot on the roof and the dot on the ceiling. These should line up fairly well.

15 Cut a 6" (15cm) piece of wire. Make a spiral with one end of the wire by gripping one end with needle-nose pliers and turning the wire around the pliers.

16 Thread a bead onto the wire and then thread the wire down through both holes so the spiral rests on the bead that rests on the roof. Attach a jump ring to the fairy's wing. Lay your house on its back. String enough beads on the wire you poked through the roof to cover the wire from the ceiling down to the fairy's wing. Twist the end of the wire into a U shape to hold the beads on and thread the wing jump ring onto the wire.

17 Wrap the wire around itself several times to secure. Repeat steps 8–17 for more fairies, if desired.

INCHIES

This week is a bit of a breather in terms of techniques. You will be using inchies—that is, a scrap of paper that measures 1" (3cm) square. For your inchies, use some of the scraps that you have accumulated over the past few weeks. For these projects, what you gain in ease, you lose in time. You have to work fast and furious to complete all three projects in a week.

CHALLENGES

Poetry

Get a book of children's poetry. Read it to your children for a few nights instead of a bedtime story. Younger children especially like poems that rhyme or that are about other kids. Open a magazine at any place and write in your journal a list of twenty random words from the section you landed in. Use these words to spark a poem.

Reread the poem from last week. Look ahead at Week 12's project. Make sure you have the right amount of lines to fit comfortably with the number of Poetic photos you have ready (from Week 9).

Photo

Capture Movement

Take photos of your children as they go about their life. Try for some unposed shots. At this point they should be really used to you carrying around your camera, so take photos relentlessly. If you have girls and they like to dance, put on some music and let them go at it. If you have boys, go outside with them and let them run wild. Follow closely and capture the sense of life. If you have older kids who no longer race around, perhaps talk to them about shooting at their soccer game or gym class.

SUGGESTED ART ACTION PLAN

Day 1
- PROJECT Read though the steps in this week's project. Get supplies ready. Complete Inchies preparation.
- POETRY Read poetry to your kids. Write down twenty random words from a magazine.
- PHOTOGRAPHY Process last week's Close-up photos.

Day 2
- PROJECT Inchie Frame, steps 1–4.
- POETRY Read poetry to your kids.
- PHOTOGRAPHY Take at least ten Movement photos.
- RESEARCH Browse photography Web sites or blogs.

Day 3
- PROJECT Inchie Paper Bag Card, steps 1–5.
- POETRY Write lines from your magazine prompts.
- PHOTOGRAPHY Take at least ten Movement photos.

Day 4
- PROJECT Inchie Mini Poetry Book, steps 1–5.
- POETRY Read poetry to your kids. Revise last week's study poem.
- PHOTOGRAPHY Take at least ten Movement photos.

Day 5
- PROJECT Inchie Mini Poetry Book, steps 6–8.
- PHOTOGRAPHY Process your Close-up photos from last week.
- RESEARCH Browse mixed-media Web sites or art blogs.

Day 6
- PROJECT Inchie Mini Poetry Book, steps 9–12.
- POETRY Revise your study poem.
- PHOTOGRAPHY Take and upload photos.

Day 7
- Catch-up day.

INCHIES

Materials List

ESSENTIAL TOOLBOX PLUS ...
1" (3cm) square paper punch
Small flat-fronted 1" (3cm)-wide
wooden picture frame
3¼" × 5½" (8cm × 14cm) cardstock
Small paper bag
Craft floss
Piece of cardstock
Transparency sticker sheet
Eyelets
Eyelet setter
Fiber
Child poem (from Week 9)
Decorative scissors
Hole punch

Preparation

★ Gather scraps of papers used in all of the previous projects—painted backgrounds, pages of old books, printed photos of your kids, junk mail and so on.

★ Punch multiple 1" (3cm) squares from your scraps and organize them into color families.

★ Color the edges of some inchies with water-soluble pastels and blend with your finger.

1 Remove the backing and glass from your frame before painting it. Paint the frame a solid color. Dry with a heat gun.

2 Paint a second color over the first color. Dry with a heat gun. When dry, sand the edges lightly so the first color shows through.

3 Lay a number of squares around the picture frame. Rearrange until you are satisfied with the design. Pepper in a few photos and words. Glue the squares to the frame.

4 When the glue dries, color the edges of the frame with water-soluble oil pastels and blend. Finally, paint or spray the whole frame with a layer of fixative.

1 Take a 3¼" × 5½" (8cm × 14cm) piece of cardstock and measure to the center of one short edge. Mark it with pencil. Measure down 2" (5cm) along one side and draw a line from there to the center dot. Repeat on the other side so you have a triangular point at the top of your cardstock. Cut along the lines with decorative scissors.

2 Punch a hole in the point of the card. Thread both ends of a piece of floss through the hole in the cardstock, then thread them through the loop formed on the other side by the middle of the floss.

3 Stamp a word right underneath the punched hole. Stamp a decorative stamp on the open short edge of the paper bag as well as on the other short end of the cardstock.

4 Lay 9 inchies out on the card in a 3 × 3 grid. Combine inchies with different colors and images. Glue in place. Freehand draw a tic-tac-toe box or some other doodle around the inchies.

5 Slide your cardstock into your paper bag, pointed edge last.

1 Cut 2 1¾" × 10½" (4cm × 27cm) strips out of plain cardstock. Make small pencil marks every 1¾" (4cm) along one side of each strip. You'll have 6 marks on each strip, giving you seven compartments on each.

2 Accordion-fold both strips at the pencil marks.

3 Paint a layer of gesso over both sides of both strips. Dry with a heat gun. Paint the strips with a thin wash of acrylic paint. Dry with a heat gun. Stamp the edges with a floral stamp or some other background stamp.

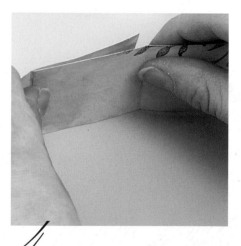

4 Overlap the two strips, one end compartment of one strip on top of an end compartment on the other strip. Glue in place.

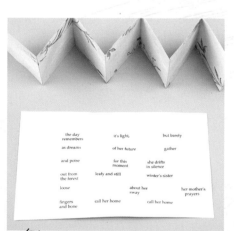

5 Trim off the far right end flap. Break your short child poem (from Week 9) into small segments (2–4 words/segment). Make enough for as many segments as you have flaps in your book (you'll use both sides of the flaps). Print your child poem onto a transparency sticker sheet.

6 Pick out the same number of coordinating inchies as you have compartments, both on the front and back of the strip. Glue one inchie in the center of each panel on both sides of the strip.

7 Trim your poem segments to fit inside the inchies. Adhere them in order, one to each inchie. If you use a photo inchie, you don't have to put words on top of it.

8 Decorate the borders of each square compartment with water-soluble oil pastels. Blend with your finger.

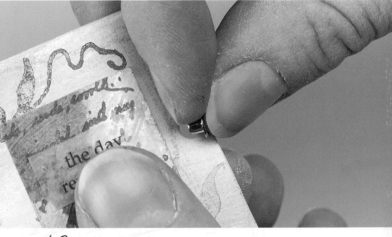

9 Using your eyelet tools, hammer one hole in the edge of each of the two end flaps.

10 Set in the eyelets.

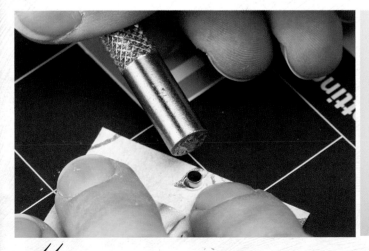

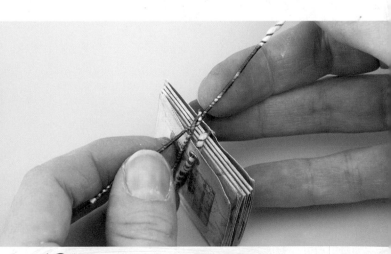

11 Use your eyelet tool and hammer to compress the eyelet and seal it in place.

12 Thread a fiber through both holes and wrap it around the book before tying it.

POETRY BOX

This week celebrates the blending of three art forms: the written word, photographic vision and collage. Bringing together all that you have been practicing these past few weeks, you will make a poetry box—a handmade personal vision that you can enjoy for years to come. This work will stand as a tribute to you for staying committed to your artistic vision regardless of the difficulties of real life.

CHALLENGES

Poetry

Reread all your poems. Record yourself reading them. See if you can find a common thread—a style of rhythm or structure emerging. Read them to a friend or family member.

Write a list of themes to work on in the coming weeks.

Photo

Ideas

List photo ideas for coming weeks. Keep photographing your kids. Commit to staying in the habit of taking your camera with you everywhere. Plan your own theme then shoot and shoot some more.

SUGGESTED ART ACTION PLAN

Day 1
- PROJECT Read though the steps in this week's project. Get supplies ready. Complete Poetry Box preparation step and step 1.
- POETRY Read your poems. Revise magazine list-generated poem.
- PHOTOGRAPHY Make photo theme list.

Day 2
- PROJECT Poetry Box, steps 2–3.
- POETRY Record yourself reading your poems.
- PHOTOGRAPHY Take at least ten photos.

Day 3
- PROJECT Poetry Box, step 4.
- POETRY Listen to your poems.
- PHOTOGRAPHY Take at least ten photos.
- RESEARCH Browse mixed-media Web sites or blogs.

Day 4
- PROJECT Poetry Box, step 5.
- POETRY Revise any poems not yet used in a project.
- PHOTOGRAPHY Process last week's Movement photos.

Day 5
- POETRY List some themes to work on.
- RESEARCH Browse photography Web sites or art blogs.

Day 6
- PROJECT Lay all of your completed projects out and have a mini art show for friends and family.
- PHOTOGRAPHY Take at least ten photos. Upload and process photos.

Day 7
- Catch-up day.

BOX

Materials List

ESSENTIAL TOOLBOX PLUS ...
Poetic photos (from Week 9)
Poem (from Week 11)
Handmade papers
Number stickers
Cigar box or similar
Fibers

Preparation

⋆ Choose your color scheme and
handmade papers.

⋆ Resize the photos and poem to fit
comfortably on the handmade paper
backgrounds.

⋆ Organize your craft space and get out
supplies you need for this project.

1 Print the photos and words onto matte photo paper.
Trim the photos and cut the poem into a series of lines
(the same number as there are photos minus one photo
that will go on the box lid).

2 Prepare your handmade papers by
gessoing, painting and decorating them
with water-soluble oil pastels and stamps
as you see fit. Trim all the papers to fit
comfortably inside the box.

3 Rummage through your art stash for coordinating scraps
of background papers, magazine images, scrapbook papers, old
book pages, hole-punched images and so on.

4 Compose your individual papers with the photos and poem lines and other torn pieces of paper by laying them out before you on your work surface, or floor if need be (save one photo for the lid of your box). Move the pieces around until you have a pleasing composition on each individual background. Make sure to number your pages; I did so with number stickers (gently lay them down so they are not completely stuck until you are sure your composition is ready). Leave overnight.

5 Revisit your compositions, make any changes and glue and stick everything in place. Decorate the interior and lid of the box. Fill the box with extra little treasures. Tie the loose poetry pages in a bundle and lay them in the box. Close the lid and be proud.

THE END IS JUST THE BEGINNING

Congratulations on completing this workshop! If you created all twelve projects, whether in twelve weeks or twelve months, you have done something important, both for you and your family. I hope that you enjoyed the experience and learned something along the way, whether a new way to look at your life or a new way to organize your days or even a new technique.

Take a few days off. Reward yourself—you deserve it! Then I encourage you to keep your art going. Reserve that hour a day or three days a week for creating. Join an art group or online forum; start an art blog to show off your creations; send them in to a magazine; teach your children what you have learned. Continue to record the details of your life as a mother. These days are fleeting and now is the time to capture those authentic moments.

You have begun a beautiful journey, but on the path you will have up and down days. If you feel discouraged, talk about it with your spouse or art friend or write your feelings in a journal (and decorate the cover and pages while you are at it). Just don't give up. Your artistic muscles need exercise and your family needs you to be content and happy. Your skills will improve with time and effort. Stay the course.

And turn the page for one last bit of inspiration from another artistic mother, Audrey Hernandez.

NUMBER OF CHILDREN: *1*
AGE: *5*
WORK TIME: *Evening*
NUMBER OF HRS/WEEK: *15*
STUDIO LOCATION: *Spare room*
TYPE OF ART: *Mixed media*
WEB SITE: *www.smallcreations.blogspot.com*

Artist Spotlight
Audrey Hernandez

Audrey is a prolific artist who creates art for herself, her family and for Stampington & Company and other design companies. Her vision as an artist is profoundly affected by her love for family and especially for her son, Montana. For Audrey, creating art is a luxury. It is time in which she can relax and have fun and express her vision of life in her sublime mixed-media art. She spends her days with her husband Rick and Montana, making sure she doesn't miss out on any moments with them. They always come first, Audrey insists. "Art," she says, "can wait." So it is at night when everyone else is asleep that Audrey goes to her studio to create. That is her alone time and relaxation time. Fortunately, Audrey happens to be a night owl and can stay up extremely late and still get up early.

Audrey's creative space is a spare room with every square inch of space accounted for. She has a desk to work from and a wall of stamps within easy reach. Once in a while, she takes the time to clean her space up lest it "look like a tornado came through!" When she orders and arranges her creative space, she feels she has a fresh start and a clean slate on which to begin a new project.

Art is never far from Audrey's mind. During the day, she mulls over art ideas, jotting down notes and planning what she wants to work on next. When she makes it into her studio, she usually knows the theme of what she wants to create. She then takes a little time to gather the supplies that she thinks might work, rummaging through piles of scrap art from previous projects that she keeps on her desk. Then she gets to work layering stamped images, antique photos, fabrics and decorated papers on anything from cards to wood.

Art has become something that Audrey and Montana can do together. A few years ago Audrey devoted some space in her art studio as Montana's work place. This allows her to do bits of art throughout the day while he works at his own little art table. Now, his little slivers of paper cover the floor, just like hers.

To his mom's immense satisfaction, Montana loves to draw and color and just create. He has all kinds of pens, pencils, markers and art kits with which to play. He even likes to use his Momma's rubber stamps and ink pads. Audrey feels happiest watching him create and seeing how free and effortless it is for him to rapidly fill a big piece of white paper. Such childlike freedom in art is infectious and inspiring for Audrey.

AUDREY'S ADVICE FOR MOTHERS WHO WANT TO DO ART:

"I would say to try and have some art time with your child where you both can work on your own thing."

Resources

Photography

Instructional Books

The Digital Photography Book
by Scott Kelby

Learning to See Creatively
by Bryan Peterson

Understanding Exposure
by Bryan Peterson

Photographing Children Photo Workshop
by Ginny Felch and Allison Tyler Jones

Internet

B&H PHOTO VIDEO
www.bhphotovideo.com

Flickr
www.flickr.com

JPG Magazine
www.jpgmag.com

Mixed Media

Art Supplies

MISTER ART
www.misterart.com

BLICK ART MATERIALS
www.dickblick.com

RANGER INK AND INNOVATIVE
CRAFT PRODUCTS
www.rangerink.com

STAMPINGTON & COMPANY
www.stampington.com

STAMPIN' UP!
www.stampinup.com

7GYPSIES
www.sevengypsies.com

PORTFOLIO SERIES
www.portfolioseries.com/product/
pastel.cfm
Water-soluble oil pastels

GOLDEN ARTIST COLORS
www.goldenpaints.com
Gesso, liquid glue and acrylic paint

PLAID
www.plaidonline.com
Mod Podge

HEAT IT™ CRAFT TOOL
www.rangerink.com/products/prod_
tools_heatit.htm
Heat gun

MAKING MEMORIES
www.makingmemories.com
Eyelet-setting tools, eyelets, cutting
mats, craft knives

KRYLON
www.krylon.com
Spray sealer

RANGER
www.rangerink.com
Distress ink pads

SINGER
www.singerco.com
Sewing machines and supplies

WESTRIM CRAFTS
www.creativityinc.com/westrim
Jewelry wire, wire tools

MELISSA & DOUG
www.melissaanddoug.com
Wooden boxes

Poetry

Instructional Books

The Poetry Home Repair Manual
by Ted Kooser

Creating Poetry by John Drury

Understanding Poetry by Cleanth Brooks
and Robert Penn Warren

Poets

Billy Collins
Claudia Emerson
Rhina Espaillat
B.H. Fairchild
Dana Gioia
Rachel Hadas
Seamus Heaney
Donald Justice
Ted Kooser
Maxine Kumin
Heather McHugh
Robert Pinsky
Gjertrud Schnackenberg
Charles Simic
A.E. Stallings
Anne Stevenson
Don Welch

Good Poems anthology
by Garrison Keillor

*The Poets' Corner: The One-and-Only
Poetry Book for the Whole Family*
by John Lithgow

(Many thanks to B.H. Fairchild
for suggestions)

Internet

POETRY FOUNDATION
www.poetryfoundation.org

THE WRITER'S ALMANAC WITH
GARRISON KEILLOR
http://writersalmanac.publicradio.org

FROM THE FISHOUSE
www.fishousepoems.org

POEMHUNTER.COM
www.poemhunter.com

Index

The Art of Personal Imagery
by Corey Moortgat

The Art of Personal Imagery offers a new approach to collage that blends traditional techniques with methods of chronicling life events. The result is innovative, fresh and meaningful collage that uses modern photos, vintage images and personal writing to commemorate everything from special occasions to extraordinary everydays. With step-by-step instructions and photos for countless techniques and 9 intensive projects, Corey Moortgat teaches you the secrets behind the distinctive multi-layered look of her collage. Learn techniques that will help you achieve your own trademark style and discover your own personal symbols and icons!

paperback | 128 pages | ISBN-10: 1-58180-990-5 | ISBN-13: 978-1-58180-990-9 | Z0937

Creative Awakenings
by Sheri Gaynor

What if you could unlatch the doors to your heart and allow yourself to explore hopes and dreams that you haven't visited for a very long time? *Creative Awakenings* is the key to opening those doors, showing you how to use art making to set your intentions. Creativity coach Sheri Gaynor will be your guide through the mileposts of this exciting journey. You'll learn how to create your own Book-of-Dreams Journal and a variety of mixed-media techniques to use within it. A tear-out Transformation Deck will aid you in setting your intentions. You'll also get inspiration from twelve artists who share their own experiences and artwork created with the Art of Intention process.

paperback | 144 pages; | ISBN-10: 1-60061-115-X | ISBN-13: 978-1-60061-115-5 | Z2122

Living the Creative Life
by Ricë Freeman-Zachery

Living the Creative Life answers your questions about creativity: What is creativity anyway? Where do ideas come from? How do successful artists get started? How do you know when a piece is finished? Author Ricë Freeman-Zachery has compiled answers to these questions and more from 15 successful artists in a variety of mediums—from assemblage to fiber arts, beading to mixed-media collage. This in-depth guide to creativity is full of ideas and insights from inspiring artists, shedding light on what it takes to make art that you want to share with the world, and simply live a creative life.

paperback | 144 pages | ISBN-10: 1-58180-994-8 | ISBN-13: 978-1-58180-994-7 | Z0949

These and other fine North Light titles are available at your local craft retailer, bookstore or online supplier, or visit our Web site at www.mycraftivitystore.com.